LONGMAN IMPRINT BOOKS

# Ten Short Plays

**A world-wide range of drama**

Selected and edited by Geoff Barton

General editor: Michael Marland
Series consultant: Geoff Barton

# Contents

# CONTENTS

# Introduction

*Ten Short Plays* places side-by-side pieces of drama which we might not normally expect to see in the same collection. Tragedy rubs shoulders with farce. Comedy mixes with television screenplay. A text for one voice contrasts with a text for dozens. It is a book, in other words, of dramatic genres.

This reminds us that to talk of drama as a single form of writing can be misleading. Plays have a huge range of audiences, purposes, styles and conventions, and this anthology gives readers the chance to explore their similarities and differences. At one level we might use it to discuss the ingredients of a good farce – and there are few better contemporary writers of farces than Dario Fo – or to consider the essential elements of tragedy or comedy, community theatre or television screenplay. The categories, in other words, are a way of prompting discussion about each play, and readers are encouraged to take issue with the introductory notes. Even if at times you disagree with the genres to which these plays have been assigned, they should provoke some lively discussions about the style and content of the plays.

As students of drama we have an especially active and creative role. When we read a novel, our minds are largely in the writer's grip: she or he, after all, creates the scenes, the characters, the facts and insights, and develops atmosphere. Whilst we make the precise details our own – giving faces to characters, for example – the fiction writer has a direct and powerful control over our responses.

The dramatist, on the other hand, is not writing directly to a final reader. Before his or her work is seen, it is interpreted by a team of people – casting directors, producers, directors, designers, actors and others. These people work creatively to breathe life into the inky words on the page before the play goes before its audience. In class, we have a similar role, making decisions, discussing, debating and arguing about the play's meaning, how it has been written, and how it should be interpreted and performed. It is the aim of this anthology to provoke you into plenty of lively discussions about issues like these.

*Ten Short Plays* is also an opportunity to look closely at how drama, for all that it can be a visual medium, relies finally on language, and you will see how some of our most talented writers use language to create laughter, tension and feelings of discomfort in the audience. Some of the plays deal with difficult and sensitive subjects. The study activities which follow are designed to help you reflect on these issues, as well as to compare the genres and styles of the texts themselves.

I hope that whether you work on them in the context of the English classroom or drama studio, these ten plays (eleven, if you count Victoria Wood's monologues separately) will give you plenty to think, talk and write about.

*Geoff Barton*

# Sorry, Wrong Number

by Lucille Fletcher

**Melodrama** originally meant exactly what the word hints at – drama with music. It was a form of theatre in which music was used to shape the audience's emotional responses to what happened on stage. Nowadays melodrama has to come to mean something else – drama in which characters are one-dimensional, atmosphere is threatening, and the plot relies on a series of coincidences. For all these apparent weaknesses, the best melodrama, as used in tense dramas like *Sorry, Wrong Number*, can have a strong grip on its audience, making us keen to see what happens next.

## *Characters*

| | |
|---|---|
| MRS STEVENSON | 4TH OPERATOR |
| 1ST OPERATOR | 5TH OPERATOR |
| 1ST MAN | INFORMATION |
| 2ND MAN | HOSPITAL RECEPTIONIST |
| CHIEF OPERATOR | WESTERN UNION |
| 2ND OPERATOR | SERGEANT DUFFY |
| 3RD OPERATOR | A LUNCH ROOM COUNTER |
| | ATTENDANT |

*As curtain rises, we see a divided stage, only the centre part of which is lighted and furnished as* MRS STEVENSON's *bedroom. Expensive, rather fussy furnishings. A large bed, on which* MRS STEVENSON, *clad in bed-jacket, is lying. A night-table close by, with phone, lighted lamp and pill bottles. A mantel, with clock, right. A closed door, right. A window, with curtains closed, rear. The set is lit by one lamp on night-table. It is enclosed by three flats. Beyond this central set, the stage, on either side, is in darkness.*

MRS STEVENSON *is dialling a number on phone, as curtain rises. She listens to phone, slams down receiver in irritation. As she does so, we hear sound of a train roaring by in the distance. She reaches for her pill bottle, pours herself a glass of water, shakes out pill, swallows it, then reaches for phone again, dials number nervously.* SOUND: *Number being dialled on phone: Busy signal.*

MRS STEVENSON (*A querulous, self-centred neurotic*) Oh – dear! (*Slams down receiver. Dials* OPERATOR)

*A spotlight, left of side flat, picks up out of peripheral darkness, figure of* 1ST OPERATOR *sitting with headphones at small table. If spotlight not available, use flashlight, clicked on by* 1ST OPERATOR, *illumining her face.*

OPERATOR Your call, please?

MRS STEVENSON Operator? I have been dialling Murray Hill 4-0098 now for the last three-quarters of an hour, and the line is always busy. But I don't see how it *could* be busy that long. Will you try it for me, please?

OPERATOR Murray Hill 4-0098? One moment, please. (*She makes gesture of plugging in call through a switchboard*)

MRS STEVENSON I don't see how it could be busy all this time. It's my husband's office. He's working late tonight, and I'm all alone here in the house. My health is very poor – and I've been feeling so nervous all day....

OPERATOR Ringing Murray Hill 4-0098....

*Phone buzz. It rings three times. Receiver is picked up at other end. Spotlight picks up figure of a heavy-set man, seated at desk with phone on right side of dark periphery of stage. He is wearing a hat. Picks up phone, which rings three times.*

MAN  Hello.

MRS STEVENSON  Hello...? *(A little puzzled)* Hello. Is Mr Stevenson there?

MAN  *(Into phone, as though he had not heard)* Hello.... *(Louder)* Hello.

*Spotlight on left now moves from* OPERATOR *to another man,* GEORGE. *A killer type, also wearing hat, but standing as in a phone booth. A three-sided screen may be used to suggest this.*

2ND MAN  *(Slow heavy quality, faintly foreign accent)* Hello.

1ST MAN  Hello, George?

GEORGE  Yes, sir.

MRS STEVENSON  *(Louder and more imperious, to phone)* Hello. Who's this? What number am I calling, please?

1ST MAN  We have heard from our client. He says the coast is clear for tonight.

GEORGE  Yes, sir.

1ST MAN  Where are you now?

GEORGE  In a phone booth.

1ST MAN  Okay. You know the address. At eleven o'clock the private patrolman goes around to the bar on Second Avenue for a beer. Be sure that all the lights downstairs are out. There should be only one light visible from the street. At eleven-fifteen a subway train crosses the bridge. It makes a noise in case her window is open, and she should scream.

MRS STEVENSON  *(Shocked)* Oh – HELLO! What number is this, please?

GEORGE  Okay. I understand.

1ST MAN  Make it quick. As little blood as possible. Our client does not wish to make her suffer long.

GEORGE  A knife okay, sir?

1ST MAN  Yes. A knife will be okay. And remember – remove the rings and bracelets, and the jewellery in

3

the bureau drawer. Our client wishes it to look like simple robbery.

GEORGE    Okay – I get –

*Spotlight suddenly goes out on* GEORGE. *A bland buzzing signal. Spotlight goes off on* 1ST MAN.

MRS STEVENSON    (*Clicking phone*) Oh . . .! (*Bland buzzing signal continues. She hangs up*) How awful! How unspeakably...

*She lies back on her pillows, overcome for a few seconds, then suddenly pulls herself together, reaches for phone. Dialling sound. Phone buzz. Spotlight goes on at* 1ST OPERATOR's *switchboard,* 1ST *and* 2ND MAN *exit as unobtrusively as possible, in darkness.*

OPERATOR    Your call, please?

MRS STEVENSON    (*Unnerved and breathless, into phone*) Operator. I – I've just been cut off.

OPERATOR    I'm sorry, madam. What number were you calling?

MRS STEVENSON    Why – it was supposed to be Murray Hill 4–0098, but it wasn't. Some wires must have crossed – I was cut into a wrong number – and – I've just heard the most dreadful thing – a – a murder – and – (*Imperiously*) Operator, you'll simply have to retrace that call at once.

OPERATOR    I beg your pardon, madam – I don't quite –

MRS STEVENSON    Oh – I know it was a wrong number, and I had no business listening – but these two men – they were cold-blooded fiends – and they were going to murder somebody – some poor innocent woman – who was all alone – in a house near a bridge. And we've got to stop them – we've got to –

OPERATOR    (*Patiently*) What number were you calling, madam?

MRS STEVENSON    That doesn't matter. This was a *wrong*

number. And *you* dialled it. And we've got to find out what it was – immediately!

OPERATOR  But – madam –

MRS STEVENSON  Oh – why are you so stupid? Look – it was obviously a case of some little slip of the finger. I told you to try Murray Hill 4-0098 for me – you dialled it but your finger must have slipped – and I was connected with some other number – and I could hear them, but they couldn't hear me. Now, I simply fail to see why you couldn't make that same mistake again – on purpose – why you couldn't *try* to dial Murray Hill 4-0098 in the same careless sort of way....

OPERATOR  (*Quickly*) Murray Hill 4-0098? I will try to get it for you, madam.

MRS STEVENSON  (*Sarcastically*) *Thank* you.

*She bridles, adjusts herself on her pillows, reaches for handker-chief, wipes forehead, glancing uneasily for a moment towards window, while still holding phone. Sound of ringing: Busy signal.*

OPERATOR  I am sorry. Murray Hill 4-0098 is busy.

MRS STEVENSON  (*Frantically clicking receiver*) Operator. Operator.

OPERATOR  Yes, Madam.

MRS STEVENSON  (*Angrily*) You *didn't* try to get that wrong number at all. I asked explicitly. And all you did was dial correctly.

OPERATOR  I am sorry. What number were you calling?

MRS STEVENSON  Can't you, for once, forget what number I was calling, and do something specific? Now I want to trace that call. It's my civic duty – it's *your* civic duty – to trace that call.... and to apprehend those dangerous killers – and if *you* won't...

OPERATOR  (*Glancing around wearily*) I will connect you with the Chief Operator.

MRS STEVENSON  *Please!* (*Sound of ringing*)

OPERATOR  (*Puts hand over mouthpiece of phone, gestures into darkness. A half whisper*) Miss Curtis. Will you pick up on 17, please?

MISS CURTIS, *Chief Operator, enters. Middle-aged, efficient type, pleasant. Wearing headphones.*

MISS CURTIS  Yes, dear. What's the trouble?

OPERATOR  Somebody wanting a call traced. I can't make head nor tail of it....

MISS CURTIS  (*Sitting down at desk, as* OPERATOR *gets up*) Sure, dear. 17? (*She makes gesture of plugging in her headphone, coolly and professionally*) This is the Chief Operator.

MRS STEVENSON  Chief Operator? I want you to trace a call. A telephone call. Immediately. I don't know where it came from, or who was making it, but it's absolutely necessary that it be tracked down. Because it was about a murder. Yes, a terrible, cold-blooded murder of a poor innocent woman – tonight – at eleven-fifteen.

CHIEF OPERATOR  I see.

MRS STEVENSON  (*High-strung, demanding*) Can you trace it for me? Can you track down those men?

CHIEF OPERATOR  It depends, madam.

MRS STEVENSON  Depends on what?

CHIEF OPERATOR  It depends on whether the call is still going on. If it's a live call, we can trace it on the equipment. If it's been disconnected, we can't.

MRS STEVENSON  Disconnected?

CHIEF OPERATOR  If the parties have stopped talking to each other.

MRS STEVENSON  Oh – but – but of course they must

have stopped talking to each other by *now*. That was at least five minutes ago – and they didn't sound like the type who would make a long call.

CHIEF OPERATOR   Well, I can try tracing it. (*She takes pencil out of her hair-do*) Now – what is your name, madam?

MRS STEVENSON   Mrs Stevenson. Mrs Elbert Stevenson. But – listen –

CHIEF OPERATOR   (*Writing it down*) And your telephone number?

MRS STEVENSON   (*More irritated*) Plaza 4-2295. But if you go on wasting all this time – (*She glances at clock on mantel*)

CHIEF OPERATOR   And what is your reason for wanting this call traced?

MRS STEVENSON   My reason? Well – for Heaven's sake – isn't it obvious? I overhear two men – they're killers – they're planning to murder this woman – it's a matter for the police.

CHIEF OPERATOR   Have you told the police?

MRS STEVENSON   No. How could I?

CHIEF OPERATOR   You're making this check into a private call purely as a private individual?

MRS STEVENSON   Yes. But meanwhile –

CHIEF OPERATOR   Well, Mrs Stevenson – I seriously doubt whether we could make this check for you at this time just on your say-so as a private individual. We'd have to have something more official.

MRS STEVENSON   Oh – for Heaven's sake! You mean to tell me I can't report a murder without getting tied up in all this redtape? Why – it's perfectly idiotic. All right, then. I *will* call the police. (*She slams down receiver. Spotlight goes off on two* OPERATORS) Ridiculous!

*Sound of dialling.* MRS STEVENSON *dials numbers on phone, as two* OPERATORS *exit unobtrusively in darkness. On right of stage, spotlight picks up a* 2ND OPERATOR, *seated like first, with headphones at table (same one vacated by* 1ST MAN).

2ND OPERATOR   Your call, please?

MRS STEVENSON   (*Very annoyed*) The Police Department – *please.*

2ND OPERATOR   Ringing the Police Department.

*Ring twice. Phone is picked up. Left stage, at table vacated by* 1ST *and* CHIEF OPERATOR, *spotlight now picks up* SERGEANT DUFFY, *seated in a relaxed position. Just entering beside him is a young man in cap and apron, carrying a large brown paper parcel, delivery boy for a local lunch counter. Phone is ringing.*

LUNCHROOM ATTENDANT   Here's your lunch, Sarge. They didn't have no jelly doughnuts, so I give you French crullers.[1] Okay, Sarge?

DUFFY   French crullers. I got ulcers. Whyn't you make it apple pie? (*Picks up phone, which has rung twice*) Police Department. Precinct 43. Duffy speaking.

LUNCHROOM ATTENDANT   (*Anxiously*) We don't have no apple pie, either, Sarge –

MRS STEVENSON   Police Department? Oh. This is Mrs Stevenson – Mrs Elbert Smythe Stevenson of 53 North Sutton Place. I'm calling up to report a murder.

DUFFY *has been examining lunch, but double-takes suddenly on above*

DUFFY   Eh?

MRS STEVENSON   I mean – the murder hasn't been committed yet. I just overheard plans for it over the

[1] a sweet roll in a twisted shape

telephone ... over a wrong number that the operator gave me. (DUFFY *relaxes, sighs, starts taking lunch from bag*) I've been trying to trace down the call myself, but everybody is so stupid – and I guess in the end you're the only people who could *do* anything.

DUFFY   (*Not too impressed.* ATTENDANT *exits*) Yes, ma'am.

MRS STEVENSON   (*Trying to impress him*) It was a perfectly *definite* murder. I heard their plans distinctly. (DUFFY *begins to eat sandwich, phone at his ear*) Two men were talking, and they were going to murder some woman at eleven-fifteen tonight – she lived in a house near a bridge.

DUFFY   Yes, ma'am.

MRS STEVENSON   And there was a private patrolman on the street. He was going to go around for a beer on Second Avenue. And there was some third man – a client, who was paying to have this poor woman murdered – they were going to take her rings and bracelets – and use a knife ... well, it's unnerved me dreadfully – and I'm not well ....

DUFFY   I see. (*Having finished sandwich, he wipes mouth with paper napkin*) When was all this, ma'am?

MRS STEVENSON   About eight minutes ago. Oh ... (*Relieved*) Then you *can* do something? You *do* understand –

DUFFY   And what is your name, ma'am? (*He reaches for pad*)

MRS STEVENSON   (*Impatiently*) Mrs Stevenson. Mrs Elbert Stevenson.

DUFFY   And your address?

MRS STEVENSON   53 North Sutton Place. *That's* near a bridge. The Queensboro Bridge, you know – and *we* have a private patrolman on *our* street – and Second Avenue –

DUFFY   And what was that number you were calling?

MRS STEVENSON  Murray Hill 4–0098. (DUFFY *writes it down*) But – that wasn't the number I overheard. I mean Murray Hill 4–0098 is my husband's office. (DUFFY, *in exasperation, holds pencil poised*) He's working late tonight, and I was trying to reach him to ask him to come home. I'm an invalid, you know – and it's the maid's night off – and I *hate* to be alone – even though he says I'm perfectly safe as long as I have the telephone right beside my bed.

DUFFY  (*Stolidly. He has put pencil down, pushes pad away*) Well – we'll look into it, Mrs Stevenson – and see if we can check it with the telephone company.

MRS STEVENSON  (*Getting impatient*) But the telephone company said they couldn't check the call if the parties had stopped talking. I've already taken care of *that.*

DUFFY  Oh – yes? (*He yawns slightly*)

MRS STEVENSON  (*High-handed*) Personally I feel you ought to do something far more immediate and drastic than just check the call. What good does checking the call do, if they've stopped talking? By the time you track it down, they'll already have committed the murder.

DUFFY  (*Reaches for paper cup of coffee*) Well – we'll take care of it, lady. Don't worry. (*He begins to take off paper top of coffee container*)

MRS STEVENSON  I'd say the whole thing calls for a search – a complete and thorough search of the whole city. (DUFFY *puts down phone for a moment, to work on cup, as her voice continues*) I'm very near a bridge, and I'm not far from Second Avenue. And I know *I'd* feel a whole lot better if you sent around a radio car to *this* neighbourhood at once.

DUFFY  (*Picks up phone again, drinks coffee*) And what makes you think the murder's going to be committed in your neighbourhood, ma'am?

MRS STEVENSON   Oh – I don't know. The coincidence is so horrible. Second Avenue – the patrolman – the bridge...

DUFFY  (*Sips coffee*) Second Avenue is a very long street, ma'am. And do you happen to know how many bridges there are in the city of New York alone? Not to mention Brooklyn, Staten Island, Queens and the Bronx? And how do you know there isn't some little house out on Staten Island – on some little Second Avenue you never heard about? (*A long gulp of coffee*) How do you know they were even talking about New York at all?

MRS STEVENSON   But I heard the call on the New York dialling system.

DUFFY  How do you know it wasn't a long distance call you overheard? Telephones are funny things. (*He sets down coffee*) Look, lady, why don't you look at it this way? Supposing you hadn't broken in on that telephone call? Supposing you'd got your husband the way you always do? Would this murder have made any difference to you then?

MRS STEVENSON   I suppose not. But it's so inhuman – so cold-blooded...

DUFFY   A lot of murders are committed in this city every day, ma'am. If we could do something to stop 'em, we would. But a clue of this kind that's so vague isn't much more use to us than no clue at all.

MRS STEVENSON   But, surely –

DUFFY  Unless, of course, you have some reason for thinking this call is phoney – and that someone may be planning to murder *you*?

MRS STEVENSON   *Me?* Oh – no – I hardly think so. I – I mean – why should anybody? I'm alone all day and night – I see nobody except my maid Eloise – she's a big two-hundred-pounder – she's too lazy to bring up my breakfast tray – and the only other person is my husband Elbert – he's crazy about me – adores me – waits on me hand and foot – he's scarcely left my side since I took sick twelve years ago –

DUFFY   Well – then – there's nothing for you to worry about, is there? (LUNCHROOM ATTENDANT *has entered. He is carrying a piece of apple pie on a plate. Points it out to* DUFFY *triumphantly*) And now – if you'll just leave the rest of this to us –

MRS STEVENSON   But what will you *do?* It's so late – it's nearly eleven o'clock.

DUFFY   (*Firmly. He nods to* ATTENDANT, *pleased*) We'll take care of it, lady.

MRS STEVENSON   Will you broadcast it all over the city? And send out squads? And warn your radio cars to watch out – especially in suspicious neighbourhoods like mine?

ATTENDANT, *in triumph, has put pie down in front of* DUFFY. *Takes fork out of his pocket, stands at attention, waiting.*

DUFFY   (*More firmly*) Lady, I *said* we'd take care of it. (*Glances at pie*) Just now I've got a couple of other matters here on my desk that require my immediate –

MRS STEVENSON   Oh! (*She slams down receiver hard*) Idiot. (DUFFY, *listening at phone, hangs up. Shrugs. Winks at* ATTENDANT *as though to say, 'What a crazy character!' Attacks his pie as spotlight fades out.* MRS STEVENSON, *in bed, looking at phone nervously*) Now – why did I do that? Now – he'll think I *am* a fool. (*She sits there tensely, then throws herself back against pillows, lies there a moment, whimpering with self-pity*) Oh – why doesn't Elbert come home? *Why* doesn't he?

*We hear sound of train roaring by in the distance. She sits up reaching for phone. Sound of dialling operator. Spotlight picks up* 2ND OPERATOR, *seated right.*

OPERATOR   Your call, please?

MRS STEVENSON   Operator – for Heaven's sake – will you ring that Murray Hill 4-0098 number again? I can't think what's keeping him so long.

OPERATOR   Ringing Murray Hill 4-0098. (*Rings. Busy signal*) The line is busy. Shall I –

MRS STEVENSON   (*Nastily*) I can hear it. You don't have to tell me. I know it's busy. (*Slams down receiver. Spotlight fades off on* 2ND OPERATOR. MRS STEVENSON *sinks back against pillows again, whimpering to herself fretfully. She glances at clock, then turning, punches her pillows up, trying to make herself comfortable. But she isn't. Whimpers to herself as she squirms restlessly in bed*) If I could only get out of this bed for a little while. If I could get a breath of fresh air – or just lean out the window – and see the street. . . . (*She sighs, reaches for pill bottle, shakes out a pill. As she does so the phone rings. She darts for it instantly*) Hello. Elbert? Hello. Hello. Hello. Oh – what's the *matter* with this phone? HELLO? HELLO? (*Slams down the receiver. She stares at it tensely. The phone rings again. Once. She picks it up*) Hello? Hello....Oh – for Heaven's sake – who *is* this? Hello. Hello. HELLO. (*Slams down receiver. Dials operator. Spotlight comes on left, showing* 3RD OPERATOR, *at spot vacated by* DUFFY)

3RD OPERATOR   Your call, please?

MRS STEVENSON   (*Very annoyed and imperious*) Hello. Operator. I don't know what's the matter with this telephone tonight, but it's positively driving me crazy. I've never seen such inefficient, miserable service. Now, look. I'm an invalid, and I'm very nervous, and I'm not supposed to be annoyed. But if this keeps on much longer...

3RD OPERATOR   (*A young sweet type*) What seems to be the trouble, madam?

MRS STEVENSON   Well – everything's wrong. The whole world could be murdered, for all you people care. And now – my phone keeps ringing....

OPERATOR   Yes, madam?

MRS STEVENSON   Ringing and ringing and ringing every five seconds or so, and when I pick it up, there's no one there.

OPERATOR   I am sorry, madam. If you will hang up, I will test it for you.

MRS STEVENSON   I don't want you to test it for me. I want you to put through that call – whatever it is – at once.

OPERATOR   (*Gently*) I am afraid that is not possible, madam.

MRS STEVENSON   (*Storming*) Not possible? And why – may I ask?

OPERATOR   The system is automatic, madam. If someone is trying to dial your number, there is no way to check whether the call is coming through the system or not – unless the person who is trying to reach you complains to his particular operator –

MRS STEVENSON   Well, of all the stupid, complicated...! And meanwhile *I've* got to sit here in my bed, *suffering* every time that phone rings – imagining everything....

OPERATOR   I will try to check it for you, madam.

MRS STEVENSON   Check it! Check it! That's all anybody can do. Of all the stupid, idiotic...! (*She hangs up*) Oh – what's the use... (3RD OPERATOR *fades out of spotlight, as instantly* MRS STEVENSON's *phone rings again. She picks up receiver. Wildly*) Hello. HELLO. Stop ringing, do you hear me? Answer me! What do you want? Do you realise you're driving me crazy? (*Spotlight goes on right. We see a* MAN *in eye-shade and shirt-sleeves, at desk with phone and telegrams*) Stark, staring . . .

MAN (*Dull flat voice*) Hello. Is this Plaza 4–2295?

MRS STEVENSON (*Catching her breath*) Yes. Yes. This is Plaza 4–2295.

WESTERN UNION This is Western Union. I have a telegram here for Mrs Elbert Stevenson. Is there anyone there to receive the message?

MRS STEVENSON (*Trying to calm herself*) I am Mrs Stevenson.

WESTERN UNION (*Reading flatly*) The telegram is as follows: 'Mrs Elbert Stevenson. 53 North Sutton Place, New York, New York. Darling. Terribly sorry. Tried to get you for last hour, but line busy. Leaving for Boston eleven p.m. tonight on urgent business. Back tomorrow afternoon. Keep happy. Love. Signed. Elbert.'

MRS STEVENSON (*Breathlessly, aghast, to herself*) Oh . . . no . . .

WESTERN UNION That is all, madam. Do you wish us to deliver a copy of the message?

MRS STEVENSON No – no, thank you.

WESTERN UNION Thank you, madam. Good night. (*He hangs up phone. Spotlight on* WESTERN UNION *immediately out*)

MRS STEVENSON (*Mechanically, to phone*) Good night. (*She hangs up slowly. Suddenly bursting into*) No – no – it isn't true! He couldn't do it! Not when he knows I'll be all alone. It's some trick – some fiendish . . .

*We hear sound of train roaring by outside. She half rises in bed, in panic, glaring toward curtains. Her movements are frenzied. She beats with her knuckles on bed, then suddenly stops, and reaches for phone. She dials operator. Spotlight picks up* 4TH OPERATOR, *seated left.*

OPERATOR   (*Coolly*) Your call, please?

MRS STEVENSON   Operator – try that Murray Hill 4–0098 number for me just once more, please.

OPERATOR   Ringing Murray Hill 4–0098. (*Call goes through. We hear ringing at other end. Ring after ring*)

*If telephone noises are not used audibly, have* OPERATOR *say after a brief pause: 'They do not answer.'*

MRS STEVENSON   He's gone. Oh – Elbert, how could you? How could you...? (*She hangs up phone, sobbing pityingly to herself, turning restlessly. Spotlight goes out on* 4TH OPERATOR) But I can't be alone tonight. I can't. If I'm alone one more second... (*She runs hands wildly through hair*) I don't care what he says – or what the expense is – I'm a sick woman – I'm entitled...

*With trembling fingers she picks up receiver again. She dials* INFORMATION. *The spotlight picks up* INFORMATION OPERATOR, *seated right.*

INFORMATION   This is information.

MRS STEVENSON   I want the telephone number of Henchley Hospital.

INFORMATION   Henchley Hospital? Do you have the address, madam?

MRS STEVENSON   No. It's somewhere in the 70s, though. It's a very small, private and exclusive hospital where I had my appendix out two years ago. Henchley. H-E-N-C–

INFORMATION   One moment, please.

MRS STEVENSON   Please – hurry. And please – what *is* the time?

INFORMATION   I do not know, madam. You may find out the time by dialling Meridan 7-1212.

MRS STEVENSON   (*Irritated*) Oh – for Heaven's sake! Couldn't you –?

INFORMATION   The number of Henchley Hospital is Butterfield 7-0105, madam.

MRS STEVENSON   Butterfield 7-0105.

*She hangs up before she finishes speaking, and immediately dials numbers as she repeats it. Spotlight goes out on* INFOR-MATION. *Phone rings. Spotlight picks up* WOMAN *in nurse's uniform, seated at desk, left.*

WOMAN   (*Middle-aged, solid, firm, practical*) Henchley Hospital, good evening.

MRS STEVENSON   Nurses' Registry.

WOMAN   Who was it you wished to speak to, please?

MRS STEVENSON   (*High-handed*) I want the Nurses' Registry at once. I want a trained nurse. I want to hire her immediately. For the night.

WOMAN   I see. And what is the nature of the case, madam?

MRS STEVENSON   Nerves. I'm very nervous. I need soothing – and companionship. My husband is away – and I'm –

WOMAN   Have you been recommended to us by any doctor in particular, madam?

MRS STEVENSON   No. But I really don't see why all this catechising is necessary. I want a trained nurse. I was a patient in your hospital two years ago. And after all, I *do* expect to *pay* this person –

WOMAN   We quite understand that, madam. But registered nurses are very scarce just now – and our super-intendent has asked us to send people out only on cases where the physician in charge feels it is absolutely necessary.

MRS STEVENSON   (*Growing hysterical*) Well – it *is* absolutely necessary. I'm a sick woman. I – I'm very upset. Very. I'm alone in this house – and I'm an invalid – and tonight I overheard a telephone conver-

17

sation that upset me dreadfully. About a murder – a poor woman who was going to be murdered at eleven-fifteen tonight – in fact, if someone doesn't come at once – I'm afraid I'll go out of my mind . . . . (*Almost off handle by now*)

WOMAN  *(Calmly)* I see. Well – I'll speak to Miss Phillips as soon as she comes in. And what is your name, madam?

MRS STEVENSON  Miss Phillips. And when do you expect her in?

WOMAN  I really don't know, madam. She went out to supper at eleven o'clock.

MRS STEVENSON  Eleven o'clock. But it's not eleven yet. (*She cries out*) Oh, my clock *has* stopped. I thought it was running down. What time is it? (WOMAN *glances at wristwatch*)

WOMAN  Just fourteen minutes past eleven . . . .

*Sound of phone receiver being lifted on same line as* MRS STEVENSON's. *A click.*

MRS STEVENSON  (*Crying out*) What's *that*?

WOMAN  What was what, madam?

MRS STEVENSON  That – that click just now – in my own telephone? As though someone had lifted the receiver off the hook of the extension phone downstairs . . . .

WOMAN  I didn't hear it, madam. Now – about this . . .

MRS STEVENSON  (*Scared*) But I *did*. There's someone in this house. Someone downstairs in the kitchen. And they're listening to me now. They're . . . (*She puts hand over her mouth. Hangs up phone. She sits there, in terror, frozen, listening. In a suffocated voice*) I won't pick it up, I won't let them hear me. I'll be quiet – and they'll think . . . (*With growing terror*) But if I don't call someone now – while they're still down there – there'll be no time . . . .

*She picks up receiver. Bland buzzing signal. She dials operator. Ring twice. On second ring, spotlight goes on right. We see* 5TH OPERATOR.

OPERATOR   (*Fat and lethargic*) Your call, please?

MRS STEVENSON   (*A desperate whisper*) Operator – I – I'm in desperate trouble . . . I –

OPERATOR   I cannot hear you, madam. Please speak louder.

MRS STEVENSON   (*Still whispering*) I don't dare. I – there's someone listening. Can you hear me now?

OPERATOR   Your call, please? What number are you calling, madam?

MRS STEVENSON   (*Desperately*) You've got to hear me. Oh – please. You've got to help me. There's someone in this house. Someone who's going to murder me. And you've got to get in touch with the . . . (*Click of receiver being put down on* MRS STEVENSON's *line. Bursting out wildly*) Oh – there it is . . . he's put it down . . . he's coming . . . (*She screams*) He's coming up the stairs . . . (*She thrashes in bed, phone cord catching in lamp wire, lamp topples, goes out. Darkness. Hoarsely*) Give me the Police Department . . . . (*We see on the dark centre stage, the shadow of door opening. Screaming*) The police! . . .

*On stage, swift rush of a shadow, advancing to bed – sound of her voice is choked out, as*

OPERATOR   Ringing the Police Department.

*Phone is rung. We hear sound of a train beginning to fade in. On second ring,* MRS STEVENSON *screams again, but roaring of train drowns out her voice. For a few seconds we hear nothing but roaring of train, then dying away, phone at police headquarters ringing. Spotlight goes on* DUFFY, *left stage.*

DUFFY Police Department. Precinct 43. Duffy speaking. (*Pause. Nothing visible but darkness on centre stage*) Police Department. Duffy speaking.

*A flashlight goes on, illuminating open phone to one side of* MRS STEVENSON's *bed. Nearby, hanging down, is her lifeless hand. We see the second man,* GEORGE, *in black gloves, reach down and pick up phone. He is breathing hard.*

GEORGE Sorry. Wrong number.

*Hangs up. He replaces receiver on hook quietly, exits, as* DUFFY *hangs up with a shrug, and* CURTAIN FALLS.

# Greenheart and the Dragon Pollutant

**by Cressida Miles**

**Community theatre** is a form of drama which aims to involve its audience actively, trying to blur the boundaries between performers and spectators. Often this has a political purpose – the writers and actors want to win us over to their point of view. In the 1960s and 1970s this led to the rapid growth in small touring companies such as 7:84, Belt and Braces and Monstrous Regiment, who tried to take drama out of theatre buildings and bring it to 'the people'. *Greenheart and the Dragon Pollutant* does exactly this: taking an important environmental issue and drawing on the old dramatic traditions of the morality play to make its young audience feel involved.

## *Characters*

STORYTELLER
GREENHEART, the hero
THE DRAGON POLLUTANT
TWO DOCTORS
A FRIEND
NOAH
EVERYPERSON
ASSORTED ITEMS OF RUBBISH
(as many extras as available disguised
as different forms of pollution)

*At the start of the play, the stage is gloomy, and littered with*

*various bits of rubbish (waste paper and cans). Enter* STORY-
TELLER, *carrying placards.*

STORYTELLER

We've come here this dark winter to brighten your
    day

With our tale which is based on an old mummers'
    play.

We've a hero called Greenheart, and he has a
    concern:

That the world to its proper state should return.

Our dragon, Pollutant, holds the earth in its power.

And, in this dull time of year, finds the happiest hour.

There are a couple of battles, and in the end some
    good sense,

Now in just a few minutes the play will commence.

Please cheer for our Greenheart . . .

(*Holds up* **Hooray!** *placard*)

NO – louder . . . **Hooray!**

. . . and for the dragon shout Boo!

(*Holds up* **BOO!** *placard*)

Then . . . (*Holds up* **BOO!** *and cups his ear*)

Your help and goodwill could make our simple story
    true.

*Enter* GREENHEART *with a broom*

GREENHEART

In come I, your hero Greenheart.

Right here in this space is where I would start

To tidy up our world, and brighten the scene,

Which the Dragon Pollutant has made so unclean.

Like Hercules in the stables, I will undertake

To scrub out our environment for everyone's sake.

(*Starts to sweep and chant*)

Packets and papers, tin cans and dust,

And disgusting old dinners, but clear it I must.

(GREENHEART *sweeps, tut-tutting sadly, but gets slower and slower*)

STORYTELLER

Well Greenheart is at work, and doing his best.

(GREENHEART *sits down at one side*)

He seems already tired and is taking some rest.

I fear he'll need more than his green-handled broom,

For the Dragon is threatening us with a devastating doom.

STORYTELLER *stands to the side. Footsteps and sound of tin cans and broken bottles are heard offstage, followed by the* DRAGON*'s rumbling and chuckling. Enter the* DRAGON.

DRAGON   In come I, the dragon bold...

STORYTELLER   **BOO!**

DRAGON

I've been around some time, but I'm not very old!

In fact I get younger every day,

Feeding on waste products you've all tossed away.

Pollutant they wrote on my last year's report,

But you lot can call me Poll for short.

I revel in factories emitting smoke.

Radioactive waste doesn't make me choke.

Give me a washing powder that won't biodegrade,

And acid rain by the bucketful for my lemonade!

Ah!...

(*Sighs with pleasure, but then starts sniffing around suspiciously*)

Fee, Fi, Fo, Fum,

I smell the work of a green finger and thumb.

There's a new plant here, and the floor's swept clear.

Who are you? Where? Come out and stand here!

(GREENHEART *moves out of shadows, wearing a filter mask such as cyclists use against fumes, and carrying a waste-paper basket*)

Ha! – an Environment Cleaner. Let him dare!
I've made this wicked hole in the ozone layer;
Nobody yet knows what that's going to do,
But something nasty is sure to come through.
This greenhearted creature shan't hinder my plan:
I'll smother him with rubbish as fast as I can.

(DRAGON *whistles to summon his retinue of rubbish — which can either be children dressed up as polluting rubbish, or a pile of boxes with appropriate labels brought in by a stage hand. The* DRAGON *proceeds to pile all this rubbish on to* GREENHEART, *who falls.* STORYTELLER *holds up* | **Aaah!** | *placard*)

Down goes old Greenheart, he wasn't much trouble.

Now we'll have a wonderful mucky world full of muddle.

I'll do what I like, and I'll live how I please;

You can all come and join me. I don't charge any fees.

*The* DRAGON *goes off, smoking and kicking paper about.*
*Enter* DOCTORS *with small torches*

DOCTOR 1    I'm Dr Keep Britain Tidy.

STORYTELLER    | **Hooray!** |

DOCTOR 2    I'm Dr Lead Free.

STORYTELLER    | **Hooray!** |

DOCTOR 1    We're on the same side as Greenheart, you see.

DOCTOR 2    With a little light on the scene, we shall soon set all right,

DOCTOR 1   And Greenheart will rise up to go out and
fight.

*They revive* GREENHEART, *who shakes hands with them, and
goes to sit down in a corner. Exit* DOCTORS

GREENHEART

Ah, poor old world! What hope can I bring!

We've all the despair of winter without the promise of
spring!

The dragon is evil, but he has the best tune.

To his powers of persuasion we are none of us
immune.

*Puts his head in his hands in despair. Enter* FRIEND

FRIEND

In come I, Greenheart's Friend, in his hour of need.

STORYTELLER   **Hooray!**

I have something in this book, which I thought I
would read.

(*Holds up a green-covered book called* Queeries and
Dancers)

Are you concerned that we treat our God's earth

With enlightened respect and a sense of its worth?

GREENHEART

Yes of course I'm concerned, but it's all been no
good.

I've tried to resist just as hard as I could.

But I see that this monster is much greater than me:

Its greenhouse effect is even moving the sea!

Our civilisation will be buried in layers of mud,

And we shall be drowned in a terrible flood.

*Enter* NOAH

NOAH

Did I hear someone say flood in here?

I, Mr Noah, tell you all not to fear.
I know all about wetting the world, by golly.
I had to save animals from humankind's folly.
We've had a flood before, and it turned out all right:
God sent us a rainbow, a promising light.

FRIEND

Light is the answer, a light from inside.
We need every person's light on our side.

*Enter* EVERYPERSON

EVERYPERSON

In come I, Everyperson.
Now, what's on your minds, I'm ready to listen.

GREENHEART

Are you concerned about pollution?
(EVERYPERSON *nods*)
We think we may have found a solution,
But we need your help against old Polly,
And your light to brighten this darkness and folly.

FRIEND

Call out the doctors, Keep Britain Tidy and Lead
Free.
The more we are enlightened the better, you'll see.

STORYTELLER *steps forward*

STORYTELLER

I think that these fellows have a worthwhile plan.
How will Poll fight this one? Let's see if it can.

GREENHEART, FRIEND, EVERYPERSON *and the* DOCTORS *arm themselves with dustbin bags, torches and lanterns. They also bring on a vacuum cleaner. The stage becomes lighter. The dragon's footsteps (and sound of tin cans and broken bottles) are heard offstage. Enter the* DRAGON *with a few only of his retinue. He is grumbling and groaning.*

STORYTELLER   **BOO!**

DRAGON    (*In injured tones...*)

But I'm old Poll the dragon, you all know me!

STORYTELLER    **BOO!**

DRAGON

I use what I need and throw the rest in the sea,

But just lately I've seen people scooping it out.

I can't think what all the fuss is about.

We've always had litter, so now what's new?

These ecology-conscious people are getting you all in a stew.

It's really not fair to take on in this way!

I'm willing to compromise, so let's call it a day!

GREENHEART

It is a day, Poll my friend, but it's our new day too.

We are lighting the way on a path that is true.

*All shine their lights on the* DRAGON *who tries to get away from the glare by lying down.*

DRAGON

Now this green fellow's got under my skin.

I daren't open my eyes because light's getting in!

*While the dragon is down,* GREENHEART, FRIEND, EVERY-PERSON *and the* DOCTORS *scoop up rubbish into their dustbin bags, and bundle it offstage.*

GREENHEART

Now we'll recycle this rubbish in any way that we can.

To use, not to waste is all part of our plan.

DOCTORS *bring out a 'save the world' banner and hang it round the* DRAGON's *neck.* EVERYPERSON *helps the* DRAGON *up, and demonstrates the vacuum cleaner.*

EVERYPERSON

Yes, you and I, Dragon, will have to be taught

How to use our resources in the way that we ought.

We must look to the state of the world that we leave,

And see that it's safe for our children to breathe.
Come on Poll, mend your ways, you can't always be
   winning.
It won't be that easy, but it's a new beginning.

STORYTELLER *holds up* ⬛ *Hooray!* ⬛ *placard. They lead the*

*drooping* DRAGON *off, trailing the vacuum cleaner, to the*
*tune of the wassailing song, with drumbeat. Only* STORY-
TELLER *is left onstage.*

STORYTELLER

Inside my friend Greenheart and inside you and me,
There's a light that revives us and sets us all free.
To work all together for a cause that is right
Is one way to harness the power that might
Bring goodness and mercy, and light up a star,
Like the Christmas one long ago, so near and so far
We hope you've enjoyed our tale and its end,
And good wishes to you in the New Year we all send!
Now come on in, Greenheart, and here take a bow,

| *Hooray!* | **CLAP** |
|           | (Loudly!) |

And you too, Dragon Poll:

| *Hooray!* | **CLAP** |
|           | (Loudly!) |

And Everyperson now:

| *Hooray!* | **CLAP** |
|           | (Loudly!) |

With our Friend, and Noah,

| *Hooray!* | **CLAP** |
|           | (Loudly!) |

and the doctors two,

| *Hooray!* | **CLAP** (Loudly!) |

Not forgetting myself –

| *Hooray!* | **CLAP** (Loudly!) |

this is all of our crew!

We hope you've enjoyed out tale, and its end

And good wishes to you in the New Year we send.

ALL (*Singing*)

We've played a little tale about a dragon that we found

And how he threatened Nature, throwing rubbish all around.

Your papers and your empty cans, give us if you please,

Aye and give us back a new world, where we can safely breathe.

Here we come a-wassailing, among the leaves so green.

Here we come a-wandering, so fairly to be seen.

Now is winter time, but spring will soon be here,

And we wish you and send you a happy new year.

STORYTELLER | *Hooray!* | **CLAP** (Loudly!) |

# A Thing of Beauty

**by Charles Kray**

**Tragedy** usually has several elements: a main character of importance with heroic, though imperfect, qualities who falls to disaster; a sense that fate is working against her or him; a final feeling that despite the suffering of the main character, others in the play and the audience have learnt from the experience. *A Thing of Beauty* contains a variation on the first of these ingredients: two central characters, both opposed in viewpoint and yet in some ways similar; both are tested; finally and inevitably there is disaster.

## *Characters*

PRIORESS
COLONEL
BENEDICTA

*The scene is the receiving room of a convent in Germany. The time is the late 1930s. It is dusk. An elderly nun, the* PRIORESS *of the convent, is pacing about the room. There is a knock at the door and she hurries to open it. A Nazi* COLONEL *enters. He is about forty. The* PRIORESS *is visibly agitated and through the ensuing formalities is impatient. The* COLONEL *is ill at ease in her presence.*

PRIORESS   Come in, Eric.
COLONEL   Thank you, Reverend Mother.
PRIORESS   Please sit down.

COLONEL   Thank you. (*She sits and he does also*) It's been a long time, Sister.

PRIORESS   Yes, time passes much too quickly.

COLONEL   You haven't changed much.

PRIORESS   You have. I've read about you.

COLONEL   (*Ignores the remark but his manner becomes harder*) What can I do for you, madam?

PRIORESS   I received news of my sisters.

COLONEL   I expected you would.

PRIORESS   It is true then?

COLONEL   I'm afraid so.

PRIORESS   But why?

COLONEL   We both know why, Sister.

PRIORESS   No, I don't. I don't understand why nineteen innocent nuns are taken off a train like criminals and sent to a concentration camp. We are Germans. We have done nothing to be treated this way.

COLONEL   Sister, you have been warned, as has every Carmelite convent in this area that we mean to have Edith Stein. If you are Germans, then give her up to us.

PRIORESS   There is no Edith Stein here.

COLONEL   Perhaps not. But we know that she is in Germany, hiding in a Carmelite convent. Your nuns are being held as hostage. If we do not apprehend Edith Stein, the nuns will suffer the consequences. Nineteen for one. That's not a bad trade.

PRIORESS   Why is she so important?

COLONEL   She is a Jew.

PRIORESS   Is this a crime to be a Jew?

COLONEL   It will be.

PRIORESS   You've become a cruel and vengeful man, Eric.

COLONEL   On the contrary, Sister, I'm merely a practical soldier doing his job.

31

PRIORESS  I remember in my eighth grade class a puzzled boy with curious blue eyes who used to dream of building bridges and buildings. Who used to serve early mass on Sunday mornings. What great promise he showed.

COLONEL  And I, Sister, remember a God who taught that man had infinite capacity for love for his fellow. What great promise he showed. We've both been disappointed, Sister.

PRIORESS  Are you so disillusioned that you've turned murderer, Eric?

COLONEL  Goddammit, Sister. You are not talking to a starry-eyed eighth grade boy now. You're talking to a man. An officer of the Third Reich. You have no special privileges other than what your habit allows. I am the interrogator here. Speak civilly to me or you'll join the rest of the penguins at the concentration camp.

PRIORESS  And may God damn you, Colonel. I'm too old to be intimidated or frightened. And if you haven't progressed beyond the eighth grade except for turning into a vicious bully, you'll be treated as such. I want my nuns.

COLONEL  And I want Edith Stein. Is she a member of your convent?

PRIORESS  To admit a Jewess into our order would not only be contrary to the Carmelite temperament but a violation of the law. I told you we are Germans.

COLONEL  Sister, it is not necessary to acquaint me with German law; nor confuse me with vague terms like Carmelite temperament. Merely answer my question.

PRIORESS  Edith Stein is not a member of our convent.

COLONEL  You are sure?

PRIORESS  Yes.

COLONEL  Very well. But I promise you, I will find her.

PRIORESS  But why her? There are other Jews still walking around freely. Why her?

COLONEL  Because she is dangerous.

PRIORESS  Dangerous? The woman is the most sensitive philosopher of our time and you call her dangerous. To whom is she dangerous?

COLONEL  She is dangerous to us, to the government. It is this philosophy that makes her dangerous.

PRIORESS  She represents everything that is good and beautiful, Eric. Don't you see? She preaches God's word. A world of harmony and peace. The path to a oneness of man. White and Black. Jew and Christian. Is this dangerous?

COLONEL  It is to us. There is no oneness in man. There is oneness in strength. There is oneness in power. And those who believe in her make us weak. She must be destroyed.

PRIORESS  Then you would destroy everything good?

COLONEL  If need be. When there is no more good, the bad will become good.

PRIORESS  What a terrible, terrible day that would be.

COLONEL  No more than if the good destroyed all the bad, then the good would become bad.

PRIORESS  You sound like something out of a Nazi primer.

COLONEL  Why not? I'm helping to write that primer. And when it is finished, it will devastate the philosophy of Edith Stein just as surely as I will devastate Edith Stein herself.

PRIORESS  Eric, I knew you too well once to believe this is state policy talking. Those are the words of a personal vendetta. You're not looking for a Jew or philosopher. You're looking for someone who represents something that you once loved. That you destroyed. And now you must wipe out every other

33

beautiful thing so that there'll be no reminder to torture you. Oh, what an unhappy man you must be.

COLONEL  There is no beauty left. It is false. Edith Stein is false. I don't want your sympathy. I want Edith Stein and I want her now. Where is she?

PRIORESS  I gave you my answer.

COLONEL  (*He goes to phone*) Major, call Camp 83. Tell the commandant that we have not been able to find Edith Stein. Tell him that at the next stroke of the hour, I want the execution of the nineteen Carmelite nuns to begin. One every hour on the hour until the Stein woman is found. Beginning with the youngest first. Relay that message by wire to every Carmelite convent in Germany. It is now 7:25. The first execution will take place in thirty-five minutes. (*He hangs up*) Now, Sister, where is Edith Stein?

PRIORESS  Oh, my God.

COLONEL  (*Shouts*) Is Edith Stein in this convent? (*She does not answer*)

COLONEL  Very well, give me your roster. (*She goes to filing cabinet*) Do you know what the executions are like at Camp 83?

PRIORESS  Stop it.

COLONEL  Aren't you ashamed, you Carmelites, hiding a Jew? The whole countryside is aghast at this preposterous rumour. A Jew becoming a Carmelite nun. Have you no shame?

PRIORESS  You dare ask me that question?

COLONEL  I dare anything. I want Edith Stein.

PRIORESS  Oh, my poor babies.

COLONEL  Is Edith Stein a member of your convent?

PRIORESS  If she were, do you think I could pass judgement on her? I refuse to wield the power of life and death over anyone.

COLONEL  You wield that power over the nuns at Cologne.

PRIORESS  Oh, my babes.

COLONEL  You have thirty-three minutes, Sister.

PRIORESS  Stop it.

COLONEL  Is Edith Stein a member of your convent?

PRIORESS  No, no.

COLONEL  You are sure.

PRIORESS  Yes, please leave me alone.

COLONEL  (*He is looking at roster*) Very well. You have a new nun here. Her name has not been registered yet at the voting polls. A Sister Terezia Benedicta. I wish to see her.

PRIORESS  (*Has not been listening, she is still in a somewhat shocked state*) What?

COLONEL  I wish to see Sister Benedicta.

PRIORESS  No.

COLONEL  What? Did you say no, Sister?

PRIORESS  No. I meant, no, not my poor children.

COLONEL  I see. How long has Sister Benedicta been here?

PRIORESS  I'm not sure, less than a year.

COLONEL  I wish to see her.

PRIORESS  Of course. (*She gets up somewhat dazedly and starts to exit*)

COLONEL  Oh, Sister.

PRIORESS  Yes.

COLONEL  Very well, Sister. Thirty minutes. (*She runs from the room*)

*He takes a few notes and begins to look at the folder. Sister* BENEDICTA *enters. She is in her forties. Yet her face exudes a feeling of youth and innocence. She is an extremely composed woman. There is a sense of peace about her. Not so much in what she says or how she speaks, but her quiet persuasive manner exerts a calming influence which is immediately felt by all who come in contact with her. As she stands momentarily in the doorway, the* COLONEL *does not see her immediately, yet senses her presence. He stands, faces her, and just stares for a long moment.*

COLONEL   Sister Benedicta?

BENEDICTA   Yes, Colonel.

COLONEL   A pleasure. Won't you sit down?

BENEDICTA   Colonel, what is going to happen to our nuns at Cologne?

COLONEL   If you don't mind, Sister, I'll ask the questions.

BENEDICTA   How can you torture us like this? Reverend mother is frantic with worry.

COLONEL   I assure you, as I have assured her, they are well for the moment.

BENEDICTA   For the moment? What is going to happen to them?

COLONEL   That depends perhaps on what happens here.

BENEDICTA   I don't understand.

COLONEL   You will. Now please sit down. (*She does*) You are a beautiful woman.

BENEDICTA   Thank you.

COLONEL   It seems awkward somehow, to compliment a nun. Is it proper?

BENEDICTA   We are women. All women enjoy flattery.

COLONEL   You make me feel like a boor. I was being sincere.

BENEDICTA   Not at all. Flattery can be sincere.

COLONEL   Of course. Somehow I could never associate nun and woman until now. Now I can understand the men in town when they talk of the beautiful women in the convent.

BENEDICTA  They are boors!

COLONEL  Some of these men have been without a woman for a long time and to them a pretty face is a pretty face. Physical appeal is not completely hidden by a nun's habit.

BENEDICTA  That is sacrilegious.

COLONEL  There is no such word in my vocabulary, Sister.

BENEDICTA  Of course, there is nothing sacred to you.

COLONEL  Only the supremacy of the individual. This is sacred to me. This is what makes man godly.

BENEDICTA  And beastly.

COLONEL  The two are synonymous, Sister.

BENEDICTA  You are like a parrot, Colonel. You spew the party line faithfully.

COLONEL  And you are quite outspoken, Sister. But what you say is neither fair nor true. Which is less intelligent, the parrot, a bird which repeats a phrase, or in this case a doctrine, or any other bird which says nothing, has nothing to say, is incapable of saying anything?

BENEDICTA  That is a weak analogy.

COLONEL  Perhaps. But so is your allusion to me as a parrot. If I embrace a philosophy, it is because this philosophy is original with me. I conceived it. I am the creator.

BENEDICTA  I imagine Herr Hitler would give you quite an argument on that point.

COLONEL  I suppose. But I am not here to discuss Herr Hitler or myself.

BENEDICTA  Why are you here, Colonel?

COLONEL  I was looking for someone. But now I want to prove something to myself.

BENEDICTA  What, Colonel?

COLONEL   In due time, Sister. Meanwhile I will ask the questions.

BENEDICTA   As you wish.

COLONEL   Tell me, Sister. How do you feel about the Catholic religion?

BENEDICTA   That seems a strange question.

COLONEL   I suppose. But in my field I sometimes get the clearest answers from strange questions.

BENEDICTA   Just what is your field, Colonel?

COLONEL   I'm an intelligence officer, Sister.

BENEDICTA   That sounds rather ostentatious.

COLONEL   Not really, Sister. Intelligence indicates a branch of service, not a man's description.

BENEDICTA   I see.

COLONEL   Now would you mind answering my strange question?

BENEDICTA   How I feel about the Catholic religion?

COLONEL   Yes.

BENEDICTA   I embrace it.

COLONEL   Is that all?

BENEDICTA   I embrace it with every fibre of my being. With my entire capacity to love. It is my solace, my joy, my comfort. It is my life.

COLONEL   Is this a required attitude for a Carmelite or your own personal conception?

BENEDICTA   My own. My feeling.

COLONEL   Feeling? Is this the Carmelite feeling?

BENEDICTA   Perhaps.

COLONEL   Then it is a required attitude.

BENEDICTA   No. Only duties are required. An attitude is developed.

COLONEL   I see. Sister, how long have you been a Carmelite?

BENEDICTA   A year.

COLONEL   Only a year? That seems odd.

BENEDICTA   Odd?

COLONEL   Well, I wouldn't classify you as a young nun.

BENEDICTA   I was a postulant for some time before that.

COLONEL   A postulant?

BENEDICTA   A novice preparing to take the vows.

COLONEL   Is that like medical internship...taking seven or eight years?

BENEDICTA   No, Colonel.

COLONEL   How long, then?

BENEDICTA   It depends upon the individual. The time can vary from six months to two years.

COLONEL   And how long were you a...posturer, is it?

BENEDICTA   Postulant, Colonel.

COLONEL   Yes, postulant. How long were you a postulant?

BENEDICTA   Six months.

COLONEL   Would you mind telling me your age, Sister?

BENEDICTA   Not at all, Colonel. I am 40.

COLONEL   And you have been a nun for one year only? What was the reason for the delay? Why didn't you become a nun sooner?

BENEDICTA   I was a teacher and my superiors felt I was needed more in the schools.

COLONEL   What about as a young girl? Did you, how do you Catholics put it, receive the call then?

BENEDICTA   No, I did not.

COLONEL   When did you receive it?

BENEDICTA   Colonel, is all this information necessary?

COLONEL   I'm afraid it is, when did you receive the call?

BENEDICTA   About five years ago.

COLONEL   Wasn't that rather late?

BENEDICTA   Not for me.

COLONEL   I don't understand.

BENEDICTA   I became a Catholic six years ago.

COLONEL   Really! This becomes more and more interesting. What were you before?

BENEDICTA   I followed the philosophy of Edmund Husserl.

COLONEL   Husserl? Germany's soap-box phenomenologist.[1] I'm surprised. I thought he was for immature college freshmen.

BENEDICTA   Perhaps. Perhaps you are not far wrong in that description, Colonel. Perhaps he opens the doors of learning for immature college freshmen.

COLONEL   And did his philosophy open any doors for you?

BENEDICTA   To study any philosophy is to walk on the edge of an abyss.

COLONEL   And you fell into the abyss of Catholicism.

BENEDICTA   Colonel, you have a distinct gift for shading a statement of fact to make it fit your own conclusions.

COLONEL   An old trick of my trade, Sister. Never allow the enemy the indulgence of accepting a positive statement.

BENEDICTA   Am I your enemy, Colonel?

COLONEL   I don't know, Sister. I hope to find out.

BENEDICTA   Then I am guilty until proven innocent?

COLONEL   Guilty? Of what, Sister?

BENEDICTA   I don't know Colonel, *I* hope to find out.

*They both laugh*

COLONEL   Very good, Sister. You've won the point, but I've won my bet.

BENEDICTA   Bet, Colonel?

COLONEL   Yes. You know Field Major Wollman, your military governor?

[1] a scientist who studies the development of the human consciousness

BENEDICTA    Only by sight. He has been here visiting.

COLONEL    Well, he knows you. When he found I was coming here, he said 'Watch that Benedicta, the brooding one, she never smiles.'

BENEDICTA    He wasn't very gallant.

COLONEL    I defended you, Sister. I defended woman-kind. I said there wasn't a woman alive who never smiles. So we bet on it.

BENEDICTA    And you won.

COLONEL    Didn't I?

BENEDICTA    Colonel, I find you most amazing. You are a high officer investigating our convent for some seemingly important reason and you spend the time making small talk. I find it most pleasant, but I'm sure we both have more important things to do.

COLONEL    You never let your guard down for a moment, do you Sister? (*She doesn't answer*) Very well. Sister, phenomonology is not a common religion handed down from parent to child. Were you always an advocate of Husserl?

BENEDICTA    Before I studied Edmund Husserl's philosophy I was an atheist.

COLONEL    Were your parents atheists?

BENEDICTA    I was an orphan. Colonel, I am aware that you have a file of biographical material concerning me. Are you trying to get me to make a mistake and give you information which differs from that in my file?

COLONEL    No, Sister. As a matter of fact, the reason for my questioning is for the lack of information in your file. There seems to be very little of anything concerning your life prior to your entering this convent. This is quite unusual. Of course all the information you give me will be checked. Therefore, I should caution you to be accurate as well as truthful. (*He reads from file*) You were an orphan in the town of Augsburg, raised by grandparents who are now deceased. Other school records were destroyed in a fire in that community some ten years ago. If you were a criminal, that would be a very convenient set of circumstances.

BENEDICTA  My background was checked by the papal authorities when I became a nun.

COLONEL  And very well, I should imagine. I understand their Gestapo is as effective as ours.

BENEDICTA  Colonel, I find your sense of humour lacking in both sense and humour.

COLONEL  I'm sorry, Sister. But I can't resist the temptation of poking at something seemingly so impregnable and formidable as the Catholic religion.

BENEDICTA  Why don't you try Naziism?

COLONEL  Believe me, Sister, I have. I don't know why I said that. I suppose it's because I know that if this room had a microphone in it, I would have been the one to put it there. But you're much too sensitive, Sister. You find my sense of humour lacking. I find you lacking a sense of humour.

BENEDICTA  Colonel, what started as an interrogation, has seemingly turned into a social visit. Are you trying to be disarming, Colonel?

COLONEL  Not at all, Sister. Not at all. Sister, you make me feel like a recalcitrant student. I haven't felt like that in years, and I'm enjoying the feeling. If I weren't, Sister, I could have you thrown in jail just for the disdain in your voice when you speak of the German state.

BENEDICTA  Should I be thankful, Colonel?

COLONEL  No, Sister. In a sense, I should be. It's refreshing. (*Pause*) Sister, before you became an atheist, what religion did you *embrace?* (*He smiles*)

BENEDICTA  Colonel, I find your choice of words as wanting as your sense of humour. (*He laughs*) My grandfather was a man of the earth. He believed in a God, but this God communicated with my grandfather through the soil. The wonder of this phenomena was religion enough for my grandfather so we did not belong to any formal religion.

COLONEL  I should think such a simple philosophy would have impressed you. Yet you seem to have flitted from one religion to another until at a very late age you became imbued with the Catholic faith and after this incomprehensive conversion, you commit an even more astounding act by taking the vows of a Carmelite nun at the very late age of 40.

BENEDICTA  You find this difficult to understand?

COLONEL  Impossible. I would not like to be your biographer.

BENEDICTA  Nor would I care to have you be.

COLONEL  At least we agree on something. But you haven't told me anything which makes your actions less difficult to understand.

BENEDICTA  Like all of us, I was searching, Colonel.

COLONEL  Oh, my God, Sister. I certainly expected more of you. Searching? For what? Truth? Meaning of life? The essence of man? Leave the triteness to the academicians, Sister, they thrive on it. I'm sure you're capable of making better sense. We're all searching, you say? What am I searching for, Sister?

BENEDICTA  Strength, Colonel.

COLONEL  What?

BENEDICTA  Strength.

COLONEL  Sister, if I didn't consider you an intelligent woman, I would think that a most preposterous answer. Are you aware of the power I have? The power of life and death, over you, over people in

Germany, over people in Europe. Is there a greater strength?

BENEDICTA   You are being evasive, Colonel, and now I'm surprised.

COLONEL   (*He pauses for a moment, puzzled, stares at her*) You are disturbingly astute, Sister. What am I evading?

BENEDICTA   You refuse to admit that you seek strength because you fear that such an admission would belie strength; would be weakness.

COLONEL   I will admit to your analysis somewhat, but I will not admit to your usage of the word, strength. What I seek, Sister, is idyllic. I have heard the vague terms: honour, integrity, sense of purpose, without compromise. I would like to see these terms embodied in a philosophy, or more important in an individual. I'm like your doubting Thomas. Show me. Show me these things that your religions spout about. Goodness, benevolence, oneness with your fellow man, brotherly love, Samaritans, turn the other cheek, show me. Just one, Sister, show me. And I will bow.

BENEDICTA   You have read of Jesus.

COLONEL   He is unreal to me. Just as unreal as Zeus, or Thor, or Neptune. Show me today, now, on earth, this thing I seek. This thing you call strength.

BENEDICTA   You are a bitter man.

COLONEL   Indeed. And in my bitterness is my strength. It makes *me* impregnable. It makes *me* formidable. It gives *me* power. It is *my* strength.

BENEDICTA   And are you free from compromise?

COLONEL   I don't pretend to be. I am not bound by ethics, because I cannot find any ethics which can bind me.

BENEDICTA   And so you would destroy what is good and beautiful in this life.

COLONEL Yes. Because there is no place for the good and the beautiful. If it cannot survive, it is hypocritical, it is weak.

BENEDICTA No. You must destroy it because beauty and goodness reflect, and in this reflection you see the brutality and ugliness of your world become more ugly and more brutal, and you are shamed. And out of your shame rise the five monsters of man's mind, fear, envy, jealousy, hate and greed. And these monsters will degenerate you and destroy you.

COLONEL Sister, *you* are preaching fear. Do you think you can intimidate me? We are masters at this type of strategy.

BENEDICTA Yes. It is wrong for me to try and reach you through fear. But it is also impossible to reach you through goodness. Through the teachings of Matthew.

COLONEL Sister, the Golden Rule is a harmless piece of nonsense for schoolchildren.

BENEDICTA Is it?

COLONEL Show me a man who lives by it and I will see a fool.

BENEDICTA If I show you a man who lives by it, you will see the strength you seek. And if I show you a man who dies by it, you will be shamed.

COLONEL Show me, Sister. Where is He?

BENEDICTA In your concentration camps.

COLONEL What?

BENEDICTA Yes. He is there by the thousands, now.

COLONEL The Jew?

BENEDICTA For the most part. But he is gentile as well.

COLONEL The Jew. The grasping, gluttonous, avaricious Jew. He is the example you set for me, Sister? How naïve you suddenly seem. Would you like to visit a camp some time and see how this paragon of brotherly love you hold before me informs on his fellow man? Ingratiates himself for a modicum of extra comfort at the expense of his fellow man? You would tell me that he is without compromise? That he is noble?

BENEDICTA The monsters are not selective about where they work. Even in your camps, or especially in your camps where a piece of bread may mean survival for an extra day, do the monsters run rampant. You see *this*, because this is what you want to see. What you are striving for. The degradation of the human being. But you are wrong. For every single victim of the monsters, there are a thousand Matthews who live and die in the strength of their God. And they will rise. And they will destroy you. This is your curse. Not the Jew. This is what maddens you. That you can deprive them of everything, even their wills, but not their faith, not their strength.

COLONEL Your knowledge of our camps seems more than academic Sister, as does your knowledge of the Jew. Are you very familiar with either?

BENEDICTA The rumours about the camps are common, and I had many Jewish friends.

COLONEL I see. For a moment I thought that Judaism might have been one of the religions you flitted to in your early years. You were never a Jew by any chance, were you?

BENEDICTA That is hardly a requirement of a Carmelite nun.

COLONEL Of course not. Are you familiar with Judaism, though?

BENEDICTA I have a reading knowledge of most of the religions of the world.

COLONEL Then you are perhaps familiar with the Talmud, and its parallel with the Babylonian law. Do you know of the lex talionis, the law of an eye for an eye, a tooth for a tooth. Is this in keeping with Matthew?

BENEDICTA   Colonel, if you're going to select platitudes which are convenient, the Talmud also says, Thou shalt love thy neighbour as thyself.

COLONEL   Sister, you know we are searching for the woman, Edith Stein.

BENEDICTA   Yes.

COLONEL   Do you know of her?

BENEDICTA   I've read some of her works.

COLONEL   She is a Jewess who, according to our information, has become a Catholic.

BENEDICTA   Oh.

COLONEL   Do you find that surprising?

BENEDICTA   I suppose it would depend on the circumstances. People have their own reasons for converting.

COLONEL   As you had, no doubt?

BENEDICTA   As I had.

COLONEL   I suppose so. Still it does seem strange for an orthodox Jewess, a scholar, no less, to take such a radical step as to become a Catholic.

BENEDICTA   No more strange than if she became a Lutheran or Calvinist, or Baptist. It is as simple as making a discovery of something which has more importance to the individual. Judaism is a moderate belief. The central truth of its teaching is that the final aim of its religion is morality. Conduct in everyday life is more important than the right belief. According to the Talmud, every good man is assured of Heaven. In Hinduism, ritual perfection is the ultimate; and in Catholicism, the faith is the most important factor in guiding man's destiny. Salvation is dependent on grace rather than merit.

There should be no standard of comparison, no competition. The only standard can be what is essentially right for a person's soul. Or what he feels is right.

COLONEL  That's a very liberal attitude for a Catholic nun. Maybe you should be the one to worry about microphones.

BENEDICTA  I have my moments of indecision and question, Colonel. It is then that I seek my God. It is then that he reassures me. It is then that he justifies my love.

COLONEL  I wish I had your capacity for totalness with an emotion, Sister. For loving.

BENEDICTA  I'm sorry for you.

COLONEL  Sorry for me?

BENEDICTA  I'm sorry for anyone who has lost the capacity to love.

COLONEL  You're sorry for me. It's been a long time since anyone has said that to me. Thank you.

BENEDICTA  Do you not have a family?

COLONEL  Yes.

BENEDICTA  And with them?

COLONEL  I feel nothing. Except perhaps obligation.

BENEDICTA  That is sad. Not to know love.

COLONEL  Yet if one does not know it, he does not miss it, so it is not sad.

BENEDICTA  Do you believe that?

COLONEL  No.

BENEDICTA  To love, one must be able to give.

COLONEL  I think so. Yet there are many ways to love.

BENEDICTA  There is only one way to give in love. Give of yourself.

COLONEL  That is an easy thing to say, Sister. But for many, a difficult thing to achieve. To what extent does one give of himself? Part to love, part to business, part to religion, part to philosophy, there's nothing left for himself.

BENEDICTA   Love is selfish. Love demands much. And love rewards in kind. With love.

COLONEL   Perhaps, Sister. But I find it difficult to be total in any emotion, even hate.

BENEDICTA   You are unique for a Nazi soldier.

COLONEL   And you Sister are very frank and open. An admirable quality, but in our time an essentially dangerous one. I wonder, Sister, if you are ever tortured by doubts.

BENEDICTA   No one is infallible. My doubts and weaknesses are a great cause of distress to me.

COLONEL   That's another thing we have in common.

BENEDICTA   You are distressed?

COLONEL   Continually.

BENEDICTA   I wish I could help you.

COLONEL   Now that is a strange thing for you to say.

BENEDICTA   Not really.

COLONEL   You know Sister, I came here to find Edith Stein. We were led to believe that Edith Stein has become a Carmelite nun and is cloistered in a convent, possibly this one. (*She does not answer*) This does not surprise you?

BENEDICTA   I am surprised.

COLONEL   At what I've told you or at the fact that I know?

BENEDICTA   (*She does not answer this question*) Have you found her yet, this Edith Stein?

COLONEL   There are many nuns in this convent, Sister. At this point I have spoken to only Sister Terezia Benedicta. You may go, Sister.

BENEDICTA   What about the nuns interned at Cologne?

COLONEL   They will be released, Sister.

BENEDICTA   Thank you, Colonel.

COLONEL  You may go, Sister.

BENEDICTA  Colonel...

COLONEL  You may go, Sister! (*She starts to go*) Oh, Sister. (*She stops*) I shall go on searching.

BENEDICTA  Goodbye, Colonel.

COLONEL  Goodbye. (*He walks to the desk and writes a comment on her file. He then picks up the phone*) Gestapo Headquarters, extension 711. Major, send word to Camp 83...(*The door bursts open and the* PRIORESS *rushes in*)

PRIORESS  Colonel!

COLONEL  (*Into phone*) Just a minute. Yes, Reverend Mother.

PRIORESS  Colonel, I must speak to you.

COLONEL  Sister, I'm busy now.

PRIORESS  I must speak to you now.

COLONEL  (*Into phone*) I'll call you back. (*Hangs up*) What is it?

PRIORESS  I cannot have the deaths of those children on my conscience.

COLONEL  I beg your pardon.

PRIORESS  My nuns, interned at Cologne. I can't bear the thought of them.

COLONEL  I'm sorry, Reverend Mother, but...

PRIORESS  No, let me finish. I've thought this over many times in the past short while. I hoped you would find out for yourself. I prayed you would. Now I must tell you. I must tell you the information regarding Edith Stein.

COLONEL  Sister, before you speak...

PRIORESS  Don't stop me or I'll be unable to. Oh, God, oh my God, Sister Benedicta and Edith Stein are the same person. (*She sits dazedly in the chair, crying. The* COLONEL *stands motionless for a long time. He walks slowly to a chair and sits*)

COLONEL   (*To himself*) A thing of goodness and beauty must be destroyed. It reflects and in its reflection, ugliness and brutality become more ugly and more brutal and they must destroy it. It cannot survive.

PRIORESS   What?

COLONEL   Nothing, Sister, nothing of any importance at all. (*He picks up phone*) Gestapo headquarters. Extension 711. Major? Yes, it is I. Yes, I found her. She is at the convent. Send a car down. Yes, I will wait. (*He begins to walk around the room slowly*)

PRIORESS   What I have done, what you have forced me to do, is despicable. (*He doesn't answer*) I have a responsibility to my convent. I could not risk the lives of all those sisters.

COLONEL   I understand, Sister.

PRIORESS   How terrible this will be for Sister Benedicta.

COLONEL   Yes. This will be most terrible for Sister Benedicta.

PRIORESS   What will happen to her?

COLONEL   She will be sent to Auschwitz.

PRIORESS   May God forgive us.

COLONEL   No, Sister. May we forgive God.

*Curtain, as he prepares to leave*

# Dead End

## by Richard Parsons

A **thriller**, as the name suggests, is designed to thrill or terrify the audience. In the theatre and in fiction the genre frequently involves murder. There also usually needs to be an element of 'dramatic irony' – that is, something the audience knows which the characters on stage are unaware of. In *Dead End* (first performed in 1991) the key ingredient of a thriller is the way we can never quite predict what will happen next: tension is tightened to the last second.

*Characters*

ARABELLA   SNELGROVE
BRIAN   WEDMORE

*Arabella and Brian are talking in her cottage. She is a single woman, still attractive. Brian is in his thirties. They could be about the same age.*

ARABELLA   I'm so glad you like it here.
BRIAN   It's gorgeous . . . so peaceful.
ARABELLA   So typically English, I always think. Nothing could ever happen.
BRIAN   But it's not dull.
ARABELLA   Oh, no. Not if you care for gardening.
BRIAN   It was lucky I stopped to admire your roses.

ARABELLA  I could see you were a connoisseur.

BRIAN  I'm not that. I'm just fond of the smell...and the colour. Deep red is my favourite.

ARABELLA  You were staring in such an interested way. That was what made me invite you to come in.

BRIAN  You'd better be careful. There are some bad eggs around.

ARABELLA  I'm sure I can trust you. You have an honest face.

BRIAN  Some of the worst are like that...the charming psychopaths.

ARABELLA  I wanted you to enjoy the cottage.

BRIAN  It's frightfully olde-worlde. The brass knobs... the oak beams...and the ingle-nook.

ARABELLA  More my mother's taste than mine.

BRIAN  Will I have the pleasure of meeting her?

ARABELLA  I'm afraid not. She seldom sees anyone these days. And now what can I offer you? A cup of tea?

BRIAN  I'd prefer sherry...if it's equally convenient.

ARABELLA  Of course.

*She pours the drinks*

BRIAN  How kind you are.

ARABELLA  It's a pleasure to offer hospitality. The village is such a show piece. We want visitors to enjoy themselves.

BRIAN  You can afford to say that. You're miles from a town. That preserves you from the horrors of mass tourism.

ARABELLA  I suppose you're right. We *are* rather off the beaten track.

BRIAN  And your road here doesn't lead anywhere.

ARABELLA  It's a cul-de-sac...a dead end. And mine is the last house.

BRIAN    You don't occasionally feel lonely?

ARABELLA   Not really. Mother may be physically decrepit. But she has a lively mind.

BRIAN    I'm awfully sorry to miss her.

ARABELLA   She still keeps in touch with the world. Through me.

BRIAN    I gather she was once quite a power in the land here . . . Women's Institute . . . drama group.

ARABELLA   (*Surprised*) Oh, you know about Mother?

BRIAN    They told me in the village. I got chatting.

ARABELLA   I can see you're the type.

BRIAN    What type?

ARABELLA   To get chatting.

BRIAN    Talkative, you mean?

ARABELLA   No, friendly.

BRIAN    Thank you, Miss . . . er . . .

ARABELLA   Arabella Snelgrove. It's a silly name, I'm afraid. But I didn't invent it.

BRIAN    I'm Brian Wedmore.

ARABELLA   Married, I suppose?

BRIAN    No.

ARABELLA   Nor am I.

BRIAN    It's a pity your mother can't get out more.

ARABELLA   She does go sometimes.

BRIAN    She's never seen in the village.

ARABELLA   How do you know?

BRIAN    They told me.

ARABELLA   Mother takes little walks after dark.

BRIAN    How strange. Why is that?

ARABELLA   She doesn't like people looking at her.

BRIAN    Self-conscious, perhaps?

ARABELLA   In a way.

BRIAN    That's funny. She used to run the Women's Institute. They must have looked at her then.

ARABELLA   She has changed. She's quite old, you know.

54

BRIAN   Fading mentally, maybe?

ARABELLA   Not in the least. Just withdrawing a bit.

BRIAN   How long is it since anyone saw her? Other than yourself?

ARABELLA   A little time, I suppose.

BRIAN   Three or four years, they said.

ARABELLA   It could be that.

BRIAN   You would expect the doctor to call.

ARABELLA   She doesn't want him. She's not ill. Being elderly is not an illness. You'll find that out yourself one day... if you live to be old.

BRIAN   Doesn't he try to come, all the same?

ARABELLA   Yes, but she won't have him.

BRIAN   It only takes a skip of the heart beat. If anything happened, it would be awkward. For the doctor, I mean.

ARABELLA   I don't see why.

BRIAN   He should have examined her. It would help with the Death Certificate.

ARABELLA   That hasn't arisen yet.

BRIAN   It must be inconvenient sometimes. Your mother refusing to go out in the daytime. For example, I suppose she's entitled to some form of pension. How does she draw that?

ARABELLA   It comes by post.

BRIAN   Aren't there sometimes things to sign?

ARABELLA   I do that for her. Her fingers are a bit unreliable. Nobody seems to mind.

BRIAN   They might mind.

ARABELLA   Mind what?

BRIAN   If things were wrong.

ARABELLA   What could be wrong?

BRIAN   Nowadays there is a lot of fraud, I'm afraid. People claiming benefits they're not entitled to.

ARABELLA  But of course Mother is entitled to a pension. In fact she has three.

BRIAN  Three?

ARABELLA  There's the pension from the State... everyone gets that. Then there's a pension from my late father's company. And Mother also receives an annuity. She bought it with her savings.

BRIAN  They all die with her?

ARABELLA  I suppose so.

BRIAN  That will be a sad day for you.

ARABELLA  Well, of course.

BRIAN  I was thinking of the loss of the three pensions.

ARABELLA  I should be all right. I would be free to take a job then. And I have a bit of money of my own...and some good jewellery. It was left by an aunt.

BRIAN  How fortunate.

ARABELLA  My sister wasn't at all pleased at the time. Mind you, she was twenty years older than me.

BRIAN  As much as that?

ARABELLA  Yes, my father had been based abroad. Soon after he retired at fifty, I was born. My mother was over forty and my sister was already married.

BRIAN  I see.

ARABELLA  I'm afraid I was always spoilt, so when my aunt died and left me the jewellery, my sister said it ought to have been divided. She's dead now, poor thing. We rather lost touch. The family didn't much care for her husband.

BRIAN  So you have no other relations?

ARABELLA  I've got a nephew...my sister's son. He can't be much younger than me. He lives in the North. I haven't seen him since we were children. I shouldn't recognise him if I met him now.

BRIAN  What a pity he can't come and see you.

ARABELLA   I don't know that I should like that. When he was a boy he used to do...well...rather cruel things.

BRIAN   He's still your flesh and blood.

ARABELLA   I suppose so. Anyway, the family feud will be made up one day. I've left my nephew everything I possess. It seemed only fair.

BRIAN   But you could get married?

ARABELLA   I don't think so. But even if I did, I feel my aunt's legacy should go to my nephew. He'll have to wait for it a long time, I hope.

BRIAN   I'm glad you've got a bit of money.

ARABELLA   Why is that, Mr Wedmore?

BRIAN   It helps to allay suspicion.

ARABELLA   I don't understand.

BRIAN   You know how tongues wag in a village.

ARABELLA   I don't really. We keep rather aloof ...because of Mother.

BRIAN   That's the point. She's never seen. How do they know she is still alive?

ARABELLA   It's none of their business.

BRIAN   They think it is...at the Post Office, even though the pension comes by post. There are stringent penalties for concealing a death. It would be fraudulent to go on drawing the pension after that.

ARABELLA   But of course. I should never think of doing so.

BRIAN   We live, unfortunately, in an age of suspicion.

ARABELLA   (*Annoyed*) So it would seem.

BRIAN   Few of us are entirely above board.

ARABELLA   Speak for yourself, Mr Wedmore.

BRIAN   Take me for example. What do you think I am? Poet? Painter? Pianist?

ARABELLA   A minor civil servant.

BRIAN   Absolutely right. I'm a man from the Ministry.

We don't wear bowler hats anymore. I left my briefcase in the car.

ARABELLA   There's no car outside.

BRIAN   Other side of the common. I thought it would be more tactful. One is trained to be tactful. Right from the start.

ARABELLA   So you came here on purpose?

BRIAN   If you hadn't invited me in, I should have knocked on the door. A firm but unterrifying knock is what the training manual advises.

ARABELLA   I thought you were asking some pertinent questions.

BRIAN   Better than being impertinent. (*He chuckles feebly*) I have these flashes of wit.

ARABELLA   What is your ministry, may I ask?

BRIAN   The Department of Health and Social Security.

ARABELLA   (*Naïvely*) Oh, you're awfully nice fellows. Mother's State pension comes from you.

BRIAN   (*Ominously*) Exactly.

ARABELLA   How nice that you can now see for yourself how well the money is being spent!

BRIAN   That was my intention.

ARABELLA   I think that's rather touching. Using your day off in this way. It quite restores my faith in human nature.

BRIAN   But it's not my day off. If it was, I should be wearing my country shirt and my natty jeans.

ARABELLA   You mean they pay you to come and drink sherry with me?

BRIAN   In a way. I'm an investigator.

ARABELLA   How thrilling! A sort of detective.

BRIAN   You could say that. My job is to look into cases of suspected fraud.

ARABELLA   (*Composed*) A snooper?

BRIAN   It's not a word we favour.

ARABELLA  It can't be everyone's cup of tea. More sherry, by the way?

BRIAN  No, thank you.

ARABELLA  Well, I hope you're not investigating me.

BRIAN  That *was* my plan. I want to be sure that your mother is still alive.

ARABELLA  You *can* be sure. I give you my word.

BRIAN  That's not quite enough.

ARABELLA  I find that rather sad and insulting too. I'm a Friend of the Victoria and Albert Museum and my uncle went to Charterhouse. You'd do better to call on Major Pawson-Smith at the Old Forge. Ask him about his television licence.

BRIAN  It's proof about your mother that we need.

ARABELLA  How long have you entertained these unworthy suspicions?

BRIAN  About a year.

ARABELLA  You should have sent someone before.

BRIAN  We did.

ARABELLA  Well? What was the report?

BRIAN  There wasn't one.

ARABELLA  How strange! and how unlike the Civil Service.

BRIAN  It was a mix-up, somehow. They do happen occasionally. Our Mr Marlow was due to visit you on a Friday afternoon. It was too late for him to report back that night. Next week he was joining another ministry in Scotland. He wanted to make a clean break.

ARABELLA  He could have reported from Scotland.

BRIAN  He could ... but he didn't. We sent reminders. They must have been pigeon-holed. Mr Marlow was like that. We weren't sorry to lose him.

ARABELLA  You could have tried again.

BRIAN  We did ... fresh blood. Mr Ross-Trimmingham

... A retired diplomat ... tremendously urbane. The iron hand in the velvet glove.

ARABELLA Couldn't he clear up the mystery?

BRIAN Far from it ... He became one himself. He just threw everything up.

ARABELLA On, dear ... How messy.

BRIAN I mean, he resigned. We never saw him again. A typewritten postcard arrived saying he had gone to Tasmania ... in a sailing boat ... alone. Of course, when you met Mrs Ross-Trimmingham, you could understand why.

ARABELLA You could have asked him for a report.

BRIAN He didn't leave a forwarding address.

ARABELLA Then he won't get a pension.

BRIAN (*Nastily*) That seems to mean a lot to you.

ARABELLA How strange! Losing two men in that way. Like the brides in the bath.

BRIAN I don't see the connection.

ARABELLA *They* kept disappearing too. Eventually people began to wonder.

BRIAN We're too busy for abstract speculation. A sense of wonder is not encouraged in Whitehall. But we would like to know what you remember about these visitors. You were their last port of call.

ARABELLA I don't remember them at all.

BRIAN How odd! One could perhaps forget Mr Marlow ... a rather ordinary person. But Mr Ross-Trimmingham had a touch of the exotic. I believe he had served in Brussels. (*He pauses*) There's one other thing I should like to ask.

ARABELLA Go on.

BRIAN (*Sharply*) Why does your garden contain three freshly dug graves?

ARABELLA (*Sweetly*) I thought you might enquire about them. They belong to my boxers ... such dears.

There's no more soothing lullaby to me than the heavy breathing of a boxer.

BRIAN   Pugilists?

ARABELLA   Dogs.

BRIAN   They died together?

ARABELLA   It was something in the stew...not one of my best.

BRIAN   The graves look too big.

ARABELLA   They were big boxers.

BRIAN   Who dug the graves?

ARABELLA   I did...of course.

BRIAN   But you're fragile.

ARABELLA   I have surprisingly strong muscles in my wrists. It always gives...people a surprise.

BRIAN   It seems strange...three dogs dying like that.

ARABELLA   There were only two.

BRIAN   Two? Well then...What was the other grave for?

ARABELLA   I thought I would get it ready...while I was about it. Animals die here in the woods...one wants to be prepared. And now might I ask you a tiny question?

BRIAN   With pleasure.

ARABELLA   Did you come alone?

BRIAN   Well, yes. You see, I'm on my way home. I'm going on holiday tomorrow.

ARABELLA   So your office won't be expecting you back?

BRIAN   Not for three weeks.

ARABELLA   I suppose they know where you are now?

BRIAN   Damn! I meant to leave a note. Perhaps I could telephone from here?

ARABELLA   (*Sweetly*) I'm afraid it's out of order.

*She goes to a drawer and takes out a large hammer*

BRIAN   What have you in mind, Miss Snelgrove?

ARABELLA  If you disappeared today, nobody would even know where you had been. And you wouldn't even be missed for some time.

BRIAN  I suppose not.

*She advances upon him, with uplifted hammer*

ARABELLA  It's always a good idea to let someone know where you've gone. In case anything happens.

BRIAN  I wish I had.

ARABELLA  Things *can* happen, you know, even in a quiet place like this. A real dead end.

*She uses the hammer to knock down the edge of the carpet. Then she calmly leaves it on the table.*

ARABELLA  That carpet is always annoying me.

BRIAN  (*Mopping his brow*) I ought to be getting on. I feel rather exhausted.

ARABELLA  But you've got no answers to your questions.

BRIAN  I have enough to go on, thank you. Quite enough.

ARABELLA  I'm enjoying our chat. Sometimes I feel I ought to meet more people. I shouldn't like to get peculiar.

BRIAN  Something tells me I really must go. I don't want anything unpleasant to happen . . . for both our sakes.

ARABELLA  You must just stay for five minutes longer and have a glass of my special redcurrant wine.

*She turns her back on him and pours out wine with various motions of the hands*

BRIAN  Redcurrant wine. We used to enjoy it so when we were children. But I thought I'd had my last glass.

ARABELLA  (*Sweetly*) Here it is.

BRIAN  Won't you join me?

ARABELLA   It will be more fun just to watch you.

*Brian raises his glass slowly*

BRIAN   A slightly bitter bouquet.

ARABELLA   Drink it up. It will make you feel quite different.

*Mother's voice is suddenly heard, calling loudly from upstairs*

MOTHER   (*Off*) Arabella! Arabella! Who the hell have you got down there?

*Brian looks surprised*

ARABELLA   (*Seeing the surprise on Brian's face*) Oh, my dear Mr Wedmore you didn't seriously think, did you, that Mother was dead and I'd murdered your friends? How perfectly idiotic!

BRIAN   Don't laugh at me. I don't like it.

ARABELLA   Major Pawson-Smith will be most amused.

BRIAN   (*Getting furious*) I warn you. I can't take it.

ARABELLA   (*Merrily*) You really are rather silly. (*She bursts into peals of laughter*)

BRIAN   (*Enraged*) Not half as silly as you are.

*He suddenly seizes the hammer and hits her violently on the head. She falls to the ground.*

Goodbye . . . Auntie Arabella!

*Black-out*

# Skin

**by Nicola Batty**

**Television screenplays** are a form of writing most people never see on the page; they encounter only the end-product. Writing for the screen contains different demands and conventions, because the director of a screenplay tightly controls what the viewer sees, using the camera to focus our view. The best television screenwriters, therefore, recognise the power of television and films as a *visual* medium, in which fast editing, unexpected images, plus dialogue can create an effect quite different from that in the theatre. This disturbing screenplay exploits these possibilities to their full.

## Characters

NARRATOR
GIRL

## Scene 1

*A blank screen, flesh-coloured. Slowly appears the vague outline of a naked human figure; it is glittering and moving like a heat-sensitive photo. There is faint music, the discordant jangling of bells, like ice against ice, growing louder. Voice over of NARRATOR: slow and languid, as if in a trance. The music halts abruptly.*

NARRATOR   (*Voice over*) Sometimes I seem to be changing like a chameleon. One moment my skin is white;

*The figure turns white*

almost transparent with cold;

*The figure turns transparent; camera moves closer to hands,
which the figure holds out before it, as if in supplication*

then my fingers turn raw and sore;

*The hands are turning redder as the figure turns side on*

but I know that my feet inside my boots are beginning to glow

*Camera shifts from hands, down body, which is turning pink,
then white, to feet*

just a faint subtle hint of blue.

*The feet are blue. The jangling grows louder as the blue
becomes clearer, sharper. Abruptly the bells stop as the blue
becomes sky, clear and icy. Silence. The camera moves slowly
down over the treetops, which are bare. It is winter, a small
suburban park with a couple of benches surrounding a
circular patch of bare earth, which in the summer is a rosebed.
Camera pulls out to reveal* NARRATOR *sitting on bench,
staring ahead, without emotion or movement. He is a young
man in his early twenties, with short, cropped hair, wearing
jeans, baseball boots and a short tartan 'lumberjack' jacket.
It's cold, and his hands are buried in his pockets.*
*The voice over becomes ordinary and conversational.*

It's sitting in this damned freezing park that does it.

*Pause*

That, and the thought of you.

*Camera moves slowly in on his face*

I accept the fact that you're gone, the cold got just
too much for you, I suppose. But I won't accept the
fact that you expect me to forget you, because I can't.

*Camera moves closer, into his eyes, which are an icy blue-green.
It becomes out of focus, and sparkling, like before.*

*The sparkling stuff comes into focus, gaining colour, and texture. It's a girl's hair; a long, dishevelled mass of silver hair. She turns. She is looking down; she could be asleep. As her face becomes clearer, she looks up suddenly; her eyes are a bright green.*

I remember you. I remember your hair. It was the most amazing stuff. Silver like when the lights are full on at Stockport County.

*The* GIRL*'s face breaks into a smile. The camera pulls back to reveal her walking along a busy shopping street. She wears black jeans and jumper over her thin, fragile-looking body. Passers-by occasionally stare or point at her hair, but she ignores them, looking in shop-windows, and sometimes smiling to herself.*

Everyone stared when she walked by, this silver hair like tinsel down her back, and it glowed in the dark.

*The* GIRL *stops as it grows dark behind her*

I could hold my watch up near her face and tell the time accurately in the dark. I could never forget her hair, you know.

*As she stands, with her face uplifted, she is bathed in moonlight. She closes her eyes and basks in its glow.*

GIRL   (*Voice over*) The sensation of the light falling on my face was more real to me than I was to him.

*Camera moves up and in on moon, full and bright*

He thought that he could share whatever I felt ... but the cold could not touch him.


*Scene 2*

*Still on the moon. It slowly dissolves into an egg shape.*

GIRL   (*Voice over*) He only saw my skin which was

smooth and white. My body, unblemished; round and smooth, like an egg.

*There is a tapping noise coming from within the egg, which shakes as it grows clearer, gently at first, then more violently*

Perhaps he's afraid that one day I will crack open,

*The egg cracks; the tapping stops*

and a rough-skinned urchin will climb from my epidermis,

*A dark-haired girl wearing a crinkled lizard skin climbs from the shell, kicks the two broken halves away, and stands face on, her hands on her hips*

and real life will pull through once again.

*The camera pulls back from the lizard woman, until she is a tiny figure on a poster for a film on the wall of Woolworth's*

Sometimes I think that he simply conjured me up from his visions of another time, another place.

*The camera pulls back further to reveal* NARRATOR *standing looking at poster. Other shoppers pass. There is the hubbub of voices; a baby crying.*

NARRATOR (*Voice over*) But when I was with her, I swelled visibly with pride.

*He turns. She is behind him; she leads him away, talking. They thread their way through the crowds.*

When we walked through Woolworth's people turned and whispered. She was indifferent to them.

*They stop as she searches through a tray of combs*

She searched through the plastic combs trying to find a silver one with which to comb her beautiful hair.

*She finds one and holds it up. The camera moves in on it, and it glitters like ice. It blurs, out of focus. Slowly the teeth disintegrate and fall to the ground like drops of water.*

When she got home, she removed all of the teeth, saying that they got caught in her hair and brought tears to her eyes.

*Scene 3*

*The droplets of water slow as they fall to the ground, blur, become leaves. Autumn leaves fluttering gently to the ground. The camera pulls back to reveal the* GIRL *sweeping up fallen leaves in a garden; while the* NARRATOR *leans against a fence or the side of the house, watching her.*

GIRL   Don't you love the atmosphere of autumn?

NARRATOR   (*Voice over*) She would say as the air grew colder...

*She stops sweeping and the camera moves in slowly on her*

GIRL   There is a chill edge to the woodsmoke...and it slices you like a razor.

*Her smile fades as the camera moves in on her face, and she closes her eyes. A tear slips from beneath her eyelashes and we follow it down her face.*

NARRATOR   (*Voice over*) And she would wince as though the air really were sharp.

*The tear falls, slowly. It shatters like glass as it hits the ground.*

Her silver tears would splash on to the dead leaves like crystal.

*The camera returns to her face, moving closer. She bleeds in places.*

When winter came she would bleed...raw cuts appeared on her face and hands like splashes of tomato sauce, and she would shake her head and turn away so that I couldn't see them.

*She turns quickly back. She has stopped bleeding; as the camera pulls back, she laughs.*

When spring came I would feel a great relief wash over and she would laugh once again.

## Scene 4

*The camera pulls out; her smile fades as we see that she is sitting on the bench in the park. The* NARRATOR *sits beside her, staring ahead, motionless. She is half turned towards him, and looking at him, though he will not look at her.*

NARRATOR    (*Voice over*) It was in this very same spot that I'm sitting in now, two months ago, it must be, that she took my hand and told me that she was leaving.

*She takes his hand and speaks*

GIRL    It's something I need, I have to do. Please try and understand. I have to leave now . . . while I still have control.

*The* NARRATOR *stares ahead, making no response. But his voice over is soft and shaken.*

NARRATOR    (*Voice over*) Her hair glittered like incandescent moonbeams in the semi-darkness.

GIRL    You don't have to stay around because you feel sorry for me or anything.

*Pause*

Please try and understand. There are no chains, you know.

*Pause*

It's my skin . . . you see only my skin, although there is more to me than that.

*She drops her eyes to their hands, her hand on his. The camera moves in on their hands.*

NARRATOR    (*Voice over*) I sat there for a long time, with her hand gripping mine. I felt – well, I don't know –

numb, I suppose, like I was dead or at least in suspended animation.

*He raises his hand, the fingers spread. As the camera moves in on it it becomes, slowly, a leaf.*

I could almost hear the leaves tumbling around us. It was autumn again.

*The leaf turns red, gold; it begins to shrivel up and disintegrate*

From then on it was always autumn. Dying. Everything was always in a state of decay or disintegration and me, as well. And her. Us.

*The camera leaves the decomposed leaf and moves up, to their hands gripping each other. Camera moves out; they sit, as before, on the bench. They don't look at each other; she looks down, at their hands, and he stares ahead.*

I can still feel her hand gripping mine.

*The camera moves in on her face*

Already her skin was beginning to tear in places and blood oozed through the cracks.

*Closer on her skin. A trickle of blood travels slowly over the surface. The camera follows it down.*

I wondered how she managed to wash herself.

*Her skin, and the trickle of blood, meet water. Then runs into the water, forming cloudy patterns. As the camera pulls back, we see that the GIRL is sitting in the bath, with her back towards us.*

I could imagine her scrubbing her back with that long-handled brush – the one with the mushrooms painted on the pale blue surface – that my mum gave her last Christmas,

*She scrubs her back; she hums and there are usual bath-time sounds*

and the stiff bristles ripping right through her white skin, slicing right the way down her back,

*As the camera moves in on the water below her back, all the sounds cease slowly*

making a deep trench like an open mouth which would gape stupidly at the shiny chrome bathtaps.

*Drip, drip, drip. Blood falls in the water, faster and faster.*

The blood fills my mind even as I imagine until it blinds me. It has blinded me to anything she may feel or think...

## Scene 5

*The camera moves in on the patterns the blood makes in the water. It blurs, and when it comes back into focus it's the patterns on the Narrator's red lumberjacket. The camera pulls back to reveal him sitting on the bench in the park as before. It's winter, freezing cold. He looks up and around suddenly, as though for rain.*

NARRATOR   (*Voice over*) I look up, imagining that I see snowflakes falling around me, but it is too cold for that. Sometime, I can't say exactly when, autumn turned to winter. The temperature dropped still further.

*He stands slowly and turns to his right*

She couldn't bear it. Last time I saw her she was crying;

*She moves into view, standing close to him. They look at each other; she is crying and bleeding.*

the tears mingling with the blood on her cheeks.

GIRL   I can't stay here any longer. I can't. This is all becoming too real.

NARRATOR   (*Voice over*) She told me, turning away as I reached out to wipe the blood from her eyes.

*She drops her eyes, turning and walking slowly away from him*

GIRL   You think that it's my skin . . . but it's not. You see, I don't feel anything any more. I have become so cold . . . so very cold.

*She walks out of shot. The camera moves in on* NARRATOR, *who stands, expressionless, and stares after her.*

NARRATOR   (*Voice over*) I bury my hands further into the pockets of my jacket as the cold begins to get to me.

*The camera moves in on his face as, faintly, the bells begin to jangle discordantly*

The air is as sharp and as vicious as a knife; I can feel it trying to cut right through my skin,

*The camera moves closer and closer in on his skin, showing the creases and marks in it.*

but, you know, my skin is just too tough.

*Closer. The bells get louder and louder. Then abruptly they stop, and there is a total blackout.*

# Trouble in the Works

**by Harold Pinter**

**Duologue** is the term for a play or part of a play in which the speaking parts are confined to two characters. Pinter's brief sketch (first performed in 1959) uses the form of a duologue to highlight the contrast in attitudes and expectations of two people. As in much of Pinter's work, their exchange begins as apparently normal conversation, and then spirals away from us under its own crazed logic.

## *Characters*

MR FIBBS

MR WILLS

*An office in a factory.* MR FIBBS *at the desk. A knock at the door. Enter* MR WILLS.

FIBBS   Ah, Wills. Good. Come in. Sit down, will you?

WILLS   Thanks, Mr Fibbs.

FIBBS   You got my message?

WILLS   I just got it.

FIBBS   Good. Good.

*Pause*

   Good. Well now... Have a cigar?

WILLS   No, thanks, not for me, Mr Fibbs.

FIBBS   Well, now, Wills, I hear there's been a little trouble in the factory.

WILLS  Yes, I...I suppose you could call it that, Mr Fibbs.

FIBBS  Well, what in heaven's name is it all about?

WILLS  Well, I don't exactly know how to put it, Mr Fibbs.

FIBBS  Now come on, Wills, I've got to know what it is, before I can do anything about it.

WILLS  Well, Mr Fibbs, it's simply a matter that the men have...well, they seem to have taken a turn against some of the products.

FIBBS  Taken a turn?

WILLS  They just don't seem to like them much any more.

FIBBS  Don't like them? But we've got the reputation of having the finest machine part turnover in the country. They're the best paid men in the industry. We've got the cheapest canteen in Yorkshire. No two menus are alike. We've got a billiard hall, haven't we, on the premises, we've got a swimming pool for use of staff. And what about the long-playing record room? And you tell me they're dissatisfied?

WILLS  Oh, the men are very grateful for all the amenities, sir. They just don't like the products.

FIBBS  But they're beautiful products. I've been in the business a lifetime. I've never seen such beautiful products.

WILLS  There it is, sir.

FIBBS  Which ones don't they like?

WILLS  Well, there's the brass pet cock, for instance.

FIBBS  The brass pet cock? What's the matter with the brass pet cock?

WILLS  They just don't seem to like it any more.

FIBBS  But what exactly don't they like about it?

WILLS  Perhaps it's just the look of it.

FIBBS   That brass pet cock? But I tell you it's perfection. Nothing short of perfection.

WILLS   They've just gone right off it.

FIBBS   Well, I'm flabbergasted.

WILLS   It's not only the brass pet cock, Mr Fibbs.

FIBBS   What else?

WILLS   There's the hemi unibal spherical rod end.

FIBBS   The hemi unibal spherical rod end? Where could you find a finer rod end?

WILLS   There are rod ends and rod ends, Mr Fibbs.

FIBBS   I know there are rod ends and rod ends. But where could you find a finer hemi unibal spherical rod end?

WILLS   They just don't want to have anything more to do with it.

FIBBS   This is shattering. Shattering. What else? Come on, Wills. There's no point in hiding anything from me.

WILLS   Well, I hate to say it, but they've gone very vicious about the high speed taper shank spiral flute reamers.

FIBBS   The high speed taper shank spiral flute reamers! But that's absolutely ridiculous! What could they possibly have against the high speed taper shank spiral flute reamers?

WILLS   All I can say is they're in a state of very bad agitation about them. And then there's the gunmetal side outlet relief with handwheel.

FIBBS   What!

WILLS   There's the nippled connector and the nippled adaptor and the vertical mechanical comparator.

FIBBS   No!

WILLS   And the one they can't speak about without trembling is the jaw for Jacob's chuck for use on portable drill.

FIBBS  My own Jacob's chuck? Not my very own Jacob's chuck?

WILLS  They've just taken a turn against the whole lot of them, I tell you. Male elbow adaptors, tubing nuts, grub screws, internal fan washers, dog points, half dog points, white metal bushes –

FIBBS  But not, surely not, my lovely parallel male stud couplings.

WILLS  They hate and detest your lovely parallel male stud couplings, and the straight flange pump connectors, and back nuts, and front nuts, *and* the bronzedraw off cock with handwheel and the bronzedraw off cock without handwheel!

FIBBS  Not the bronzedraw off cock with handwheel?

WILLS  And without handwheel.

FIBBS  Without handwheel?

WILLS  And with handwheel.

FIBBS  Not with handwheel?

WILLS  And without handwheel.

FIBBS  Without handwheel?

WILLS  With handwheel *and* without handwheel.

FIBBS  With handwheel *and* without handwheel?

WILLS  With or without!

*Pause*

FIBBS  (*Broken*) Tell me. What do they want to make in its place?

WILLS  Trouble.

# Kitty

**by Victoria Wood**

**Monologue** is a long speech made by one character. The
challenge for the writer is how to convey to an audience a
strong sense of the speaker's personality with no other
characters to comment or respond. Victoria Wood's comic
invention, Kitty, reveals her enthusiasms, attitudes and
irritations in her highly specific references to people and
places. She addresses us from a television studio in her own
brief programme, *Kitty*.

## One

This wasn't my idea. (*Looks at watch*) In fact, had it been
up to me, I'd have been on my second cream sherry in
Kidderminster by now. This lot (*gesturing vaguely and
disdainfully around*) – they phoned me up last Thursday.
I'd just settled down with a Claire Rayner and a quarter
of radishes, so I wasn't best pleased. I said, 'Who is it
and keep it brief, because I've a howling draught
through my architrave'; and if I'd wanted to freeze to
death I'd have gone with Scott to the Antarctic and
made a day of it. She said, 'It's Morag from the television programme, do you remember me?' I said, 'Yes, I
do; I lent you two cotton buds which I never saw back.'
She said, 'I've got the producer for you', so I said, 'I
hope you've sealed the envelope properly', which is an
old golfing retort of mine. On she comes – the
producer – I could hear her boiler-suit creaking even

long-distance – 'Is that Kitty?' I said, 'If it's not, this cardigan's a remarkably good fit.' She said, 'Kitty – do you like fun?' I said, 'No, I don't. I had enough of that in 1958 when I got trapped in a lift with a hula-hoop salesman.' She said, 'Would you like to come on our new programme? One of our regulars has a skin complaint and has to spend three months eating peanuts with the light off.'

I said, 'Well, I'm quite pushed busy-wise – I'm doing the costumes for the Rummy Club production of "The Sound of Music", and Helen Murchison's Second Act dirndl is a week's work in itself.' (She claims to be dieting but every time we have 'Doh a Deer a Female Deer' there's a terrible whiff of pear-drops.) But that's by the by-pass.

She said, 'Come to the studios, and we'll thrash it out woman to woman.' Well, she's as much like a woman as Charlie Cairoli, but I just said 'Suit yourself' and rang off.

So I fixed up a lift with Mr Culverhouse in flat nine. Well, he owed me a favour and he has got a very roomy Vauxhall. It was no bother to drop me off because he has an artificial arm from the Western Desert and he was coming through to Roehampton anyway to have his webbing adjusted.

So I turn up – I popped into Marks on my way to return a – well, let's call it an item. I'm ushered into the producer – she hadn't changed – new haircut – if it hadn't been bright blue she'd have been a dead ringer for Stanley Matthews. And she won't wear anything approaching a brassiere – when she plays ping-pong it puts you in mind of something thought up by Barnes Wallis.

Well – she stubs out her Senior Service and she says, 'Kitty, how can we tempt you?' and starts boasting about her big budget. I thought if it's that big, why don't you splash out on some foundation garments but I kept well buttoned. So I stated my terms. One – proper remuneration – I'd seen in the papers about Terry so-called Wogan and his astronomical figure – it wasn't my paper – it was wrapped round a small Savoy at my neighbour's. Two – I want to be chauffeur-driven each way; British Rail having gone completely mad in my opinion, all vertical blinds and chilli con carne – and the driver must be blemish-free – because I'm not coming all the way from Cheadle glued to somebody's carbuncles. Three – I must have a decent dressing-room, and not that cubby-hole next to the chocolate machine. How you're expected to gather your thoughts up to the thud of a falling Bounty I do not know. There's a bit of a dubious silence, and the producer says she'll have to ask upstairs – I thought that's leadership for you – where were you when they bombed Plymouth?

Anyway – we reached a compromise – I got what I wanted and they didn't. I've quite a nice dressing room, I have it Box and Cox with the late-night Vicar. And the chauffeur's called Kent. Kent! I said to him, 'That's not a name, it's a cricket team.'

Anyway – I must go. If we beat the traffic, Mr Culverhouse is taking me for a prawn salad at The Happy Rickshaw. Chinese, but we ask for the other menu. (*Getting up*) Morag! Tuh, there's no laying hands on her now she's engaged . . .

## *Two*

*She rushes on with bags and parcels, with her coat on*

Now I'm keeping this on because I've got a mad dash to get back to Cheadle. The Rummy Club 'Sound of Music' opens tonight. I'm prompter – and our Mother Superior's on tablets so every other rehearsal it's been 'Climb Every What is it?'

Anyway – reincarnation! The producer set me off on it. She had one of those sessions where you lie back and turn into Florence Nightingale. She reckons she's had three previous incarnations: I think one was a Roman soldier, I forget the other two. Looking at her now, I'd plump for a Sumo wrestler and a bull mastiff. But I'm quite interested in the supernatural. My mother and I once paid out for a seance in Widnes. We wanted to contact my father because we were going camping and we couldn't lay hands on the mallet. This medium – she couldn't have made contact with the other side of a bedside table. She just kept saying she could tell we'd suffered a grievous loss. I said, 'Yes, two pounds each to come in, and our bus fares to Widnes.' But I quite fancied regressing to my earlier lives, so I got Mr Culverhouse to hypnotise me. So I'm lying down – he hasn't got the right sort of watch so he's dangling a rubberised plug – and he counts me back to 1901. 'Who are you', he says. Well everything's dark. but I sense I'm wearing a corset, so that rules out Edward the Seventh. Then suddenly, bang, bang, bang, there's Helen Murchison at the front door assaulting my knocker as per; so it's away with the hypnosis and out with the mixed biscuits.

She'd come round on her way back from giving blood, and why they want it beats me, because the way she eats, it must be 'A' rhesus nougat. She'd come to tell me her daughter was finally getting married after four years of living in sin just outside Nantwich. I said 'What's his name?' She said, 'He's called Nick, and he's very high up in sewage.' I thought, that's lucky. She said, 'It is a church wedding, but under the circumstances the bride's opted for knee-length shrimp.' She tried to impress Mr Culverhouse with her elaborate finger buffet, but he sees the world for what it is after fifty years in cocoa. She said if I wanted to give a present, they'd made out a little list. Little! It made the Domesday Book look like a raffle ticket. Videos, washing machines – the only thing under a fiver was a wall-mounted Brillo grip. So they're getting this. (*She produces an awful catering-size coffee tin covered in wallpaper and ric-rac braid to make a bin*) I made it! You can't get them in the shops. I think what makes it is the ric-rac braiding. I was going to patent it, but I believe there's a lot of hanging around. Oh, and then she drops another bombshell. She chomps down the last of the Bourbons and says, 'Kitty – I'm leaving Bill – we're not compatible.' They never were – he loves opera, and she can't follow the plot of the Teddy Bears' Picnic. She only married him because he was pally with a man who made chocolate misshapes.

Now I must dash – it's curtain-up at seven and these motorways – they're forever coning you off – I blame the engineers. You can see them on the hard shoulder, larking about with their theodolites. (*Gathers her bits together*) If anybody's been sitting on my wimples I'll play merry Hamlet . . . .

# The Still Alarm

**by George S. Kaufman**

**Absurdism** is a form of theatre that frequently baffles us. It refuses to follow the logic of realistic drama and instead presents characters in situations we cannot easily explain. It became an influential theatrical trend in the 1950s, in the hands of writers like Samuel Beckett, Eugène Ionesco and N. F. Simpson. Two tramps linger at the edge of a road waiting for someone or something who we know will never arrive; the atmosphere of a tranquil French village is shattered when a rhinoceros charges through . . . none of this can be explained. *The Still Alarm* is an absurdist play because there is little point to the situation, and little explanation, except its pointlessness. Like most absurdist plays, it becomes funnier the more seriously it is read and performed.

## Characters

ED
BOB
THE BELLBOY
A FIREMAN
ANOTHER FIREMAN

*A hotel bedroom.* VITAL NOTE: *It is important that the entire play should be acted calmly and politely, in the manner of an English drawing-room comedy. No actor ever raises his voice; every line must be read as though it were an invitation to a cup of tea. If this direction is disregarded, the play has no*

*point at all. The Scene is a hotel bedroom. Two windows rear;*
*door to the hall right, chair right centre. Bed between windows.*
*Phone stand right, downstage end of bed. Dresser left upstage*
*corner. Another door at left. Small table and chairs downstage*
*left centre.*

ED *and* BOB *are on the stage.* ED *is getting into his overcoat*
*as the curtain rises. Both are at right door.*

ED   Well, Bob, it's certainly been nice to see you again.

BOB   It was nice to see you.

ED   You come to town so seldom, I hardly ever get the
chance to –

BOB   Well, you know how it is. A business trip is always
more or less of a bore.

ED   Next time you've got to come out to the house.

BOB   I want to come out. I just had to stick around the
hotel this trip.

ED   Oh, I understand. Well, give my best to Edith.

BOB   (*Remembering something*) Oh, I say, Ed. Wait a
minute.

ED   What's the matter?

BOB   I knew I wanted to show you something. (*Crosses
left to table. Gets roll of blueprints from drawer*) Did you
know I'm going to build?

ED   (*Follows to right of table*) A house?

BOB   You bet it's a house! (*Knock on right door*) Come
in! (*Spreads plans*) I just got these yesterday.

ED   (*Sits*) Well, that's fine! (*The knock is repeated – louder.
Both men now give full attention to the door*)

BOB   Come! Come in!

BELLBOY   (*Enters right*) Mr Barclay?

BOB   Well?

BELLBOY   I've a message from the clerk, sir. For
Mr Barclay personally.

BOB  (*Crosses to boy*) I'm Mr Barclay. What is the message?

BELLBOY  The hotel is on fire, sir.

BOB  What's that?

BELLBOY  The hotel is on fire.

ED  This hotel?

BELLBOY  Yes, sir.

BOB  Well – is it bad?

BELLBOY  It looks pretty bad, sir.

ED  You mean it's going to burn down?

BELLBOY  We think so – yes, sir.

BOB  (*A low whistle of surprise*) Well! We'd better leave.

BELLBOY  Yes, sir.

BOB  Going to burn down, huh?

BELLBOY  Yes, sir. If you'll step to the window you'll see. (BOB *goes to right window*)

BOB  Yes, that is pretty bad. H'm. (*To* ED) I say, you really ought to see this –

ED  (*Crosses up to right window – peering out*) It's reached the floor right underneath.

BELLBOY  Yes, sir. The lower part of the hotel is about gone, sir.

BOB  (*Still looking out – looks up*) Still all right up above, though. (*Turns to boy*) Have they notified the Fire Department?

BELLBOY  I wouldn't know, sir. I'm only the bellboy.

BOB  Well, that's the thing to do, obviously – (*Nods head to each one as if the previous line was a bright idea*) – notify the Fire Department. Just call them up, give them the name of the hotel –

ED  Wait a minute. I can do better than that for you. (*To the boy*) Ring through to the Chief, and tell him that Ed Jamison told you to telephone him. (*To* BOB) We went to school together, you know.

BOB  That's fine. *(To the boy)* Now, get that right. Tell the Chief that Mr Jamison said to ring him.

ED  *Ed* Jamison.

BOB  Yes, *Ed* Jamison.

BELLBOY  Yes, sir. (*Turns to go*)

BOB  Oh! Boy! (*Pulls out handful of change; picks out a coin*) Here you are.

BELLBOY  Thank you, sir.

*Exit* BELLBOY. ED *sits right of table, lights cigarette and throws match downstage, then steps on it. There is a moment's pause.*

BOB  Well! (*Crosses and looks out left window*) Say, we'll have to get out of here pretty soon.

ED  (*Going to window*) How is it – no better?

BOB  Worse, if anything. It'll be up here in a few moments.

ED  What floor *is* this?

BOB  Eleventh.

ED  Eleven. We couldn't jump, then.

BOB  Oh, no. You never could jump. (*Comes away from window to dresser*) Well, I've got to get my things together. (*Pulls out suitcase*)

ED  (*Smoothing out the plans*) Who made these for you?

BOB  A fellow here – Rawlins. (*Turns a shirt in his hand*) I ought to call one of the other hotels for a room.

ED  Oh, you can get in.

BOB  They're pretty crowded. (*Feels something on the sole of his foot; inspects it*) Say, the floor's getting hot.

ED  I know it. It's getting stuffy in the room, too. Phew! (*He looks around, then goes to the phone*) Hello. – Ice water in eleven-eighteen. (*Crosses to right of table*)

BOB  (*At bed*) That's the stuff. (*Packs*) You know, if I move to another hotel I'll never get my mail. Everybody thinks I'm stopping here.

ED  (*Studying the plans*) Say, this isn't bad.

BOB  *(Eagerly)* Do you like it? *(Remembers his plight)* Suppose I go to another hotel and there's a fire there, too!

ED  You've got to take *some* chance.

BOB  I know, but here I'm sure. *(Phone rings)* Oh, answer that, will you, Ed? *(To dresser and back)*

ED  *(Crosses to phone)* Sure. *(At phone)* Hello – Oh, that's good. Fine. What? – Oh! Well, wait a minute. *(To BOB)* The firemen are downstairs and some of them want to come up to this room.

BOB  Tell them, of course.

ED  *(At phone)* All right. Come right up. *(Hangs up, crosses and sits right of table)* Now we'll get some action.

BOB  *(Looks out of window left)* Say, there's an awful crowd of people on the street.

ED  *(Absently, as he pores over the plans)* Maybe there's been some kind of accident.

BOB  *(Peering out, suitcase in hand)* No. More likely they heard about the fire. *(A knock at the door right)* Come in.

BELLBOY  *(Enters)* I beg pardon, Mr Barclay, the firemen have arrived.

BOB  Show them in.

*Crosses to right. The door opens. In the doorway appear two FIREMEN in full regalia. The FIRST FIREMAN carries a hose and rubber coat; the SECOND has a violin case, right centre.*

FIRST FIREMAN  *(Enters right. Very apologetically)* Mr Barclay.

BOB  I'm Mr Barclay.

FIRST FIREMAN  We're the firemen, Mr Barclay. *(They remove their hats)*

BOB  How de do?

ED  How de do?

BOB   A great pleasure, I assure you. Really must apologise for the condition of this room, but –

FIRST FIREMAN   Oh, that's all right. I know how it is at home.

BOB   May I present a friend of mine, Mr Ed Jamison –

FIRST FIREMAN   How are you?

ED   How are you, boys? (SECOND FIREMAN *nods*) I know your Chief.

FIRST FIREMAN   Oh, is that so? He knows the Chief – dear old Chiefie. (SECOND FIREMAN *giggles*)

BOB   (*Embarrassed*) Well, I guess you boys want to get to work, don't you?

FIRST FIREMAN   Well, if you don't mind. We would like to spray around a little bit.

BOB   May I help you?

FIRST FIREMAN   Yes, if you please.

BOB *helps him into his rubber coat. At the same time the* SECOND FIREMAN, *without a word, lays the violin case on the bed, opens it, takes out the violin, and begins tuning it.*

BOB   (*Watching him*) I don't think I understand.

FIRST FIREMAN   Well, you see, Sid doesn't get much chance to practise at home. Sometimes, at a fire, while we're waiting for a wall to fall or something, why, a fireman doesn't really have anything to do, and personally I like to see him improve himself symphonically. I hope you don't resent it. You're not anti-symphonic?

BOB   Of course not – (BOB *and* ED *nod understandingly; the* SECOND FIREMAN *is now waxing the bow*)

FIRST FIREMAN   Well, if you'll excuse me –

*To window right. Turns with decision towards the window. You feel that he is about to get down to business.*

BOB   (*Crosses to left*) Charming personalities.

ED (*Follows over to the window right*) How *is* the fire?

FIRST FIREMAN (*Feels the wall*) It's pretty bad right now. This wall will go pretty soon now, but it'll fall out that way, so it's all right. (*Peers out*) That next room is the place to fight it from. (*Crosses to door left.* BOB *shows ties as* ED *crosses*)

ED (*Sees ties*) Oh! Aren't those gorgeous!

FIRST FIREMAN (*To* BOB) Have you the key for this room?

BOB Why, no. I've nothing to do with that room. I've just got this one. (*Folding a shirt as he talks*)

ED Oh, it's very comfortable.

FIRST FIREMAN That's too bad, I had something up my sleeve. If I could have gotten in there. Oh, well, may I use your phone?

BOB Please do. (*To* ED) Do you think you might hold this? (*Indicates the hose*)

ED How?

FIRST FIREMAN Just crawl under it. (*As he does that*) Thanks. (*At phone*) Hello. Let me have the clerk, please. (*To* SECOND FIREMAN) Give us that little thing you played the night the Equitable Building burned down. (*Back to phone*) Are you there? This is one of the firemen. Oh, you know. I'm in a room – ah – (*Looks at* BOB)

BOB Eleven-eighteen.

FIRST FIREMAN Eleven-eighteen, and I want to get into the next room – Oh, goody. Will you send someone up with the key? There's no one in there? Oh, super-goody! Right away. (*Hangs up*)

BOB That's fine. (*To* FIREMAN) Won't you sit down?

FIRST FIREMAN Thanks.

ED Have a cigar?

FIRST FIREMAN (*Takes it*) Much obliged.

BOB A light?

FIRST FIREMAN    If you please.

ED    (*Failing to find a match*) Bob, have you a match?

BOB    (*Crosses to left centre*) I thought there were some here. (*Hands in pockets*)

FIRST FIREMAN    Oh, never mind.

*He goes to right window, leans out, and emerges with cigar lighted.* BOB *crosses to left to dresser; slams drawer. The* SECOND FIREMAN *taps violin with bow.*

FIRST FIREMAN    Mr Barclay, I think he's ready now.

BOB    (*Takes chair from right table and sits centre*) Pardon me.

*They all sit.* The SECOND FIREMAN *takes centre of stage, with all the manner of a concert violinist. He goes into 'Keep the Home Fires Burning'.* BOB, ED *and* FIRST FIREMAN *wipe brow as curtain falls slowly.*

# Teeth

**by Tina Howe**

**Comedy** is usually used today to mean 'funny', but in literature it has more significance than that: it is a *pattern* of literature which contrasts with tragedy. In other words, the main character usually manages to escape the problems that threaten her or him, and arrives at some happier state. Traditionally, as the poet Byron said, 'All tragedies are finished by a death; all comedies are ended by a marriage.' This play has an element of this pattern in its hint of an optimistic ending, as well as containing straightforward humour in the clash between the formal classical background music and the sheer indignity of the situation.

*Characters*

DR ROSE
AMY
RADIO ANNOUNCER

*A modest one-man dentist's office in midtown Manhattan. An FM radio is tuned to a classical music station. It's 21 March, Johann Sebastian Bach's birthday, and Glenn Gould is playing the rollicking Presto from his Toccata in C minor. The whine of a high-powered dentist's drill slowly asserts itself. In blackout . . .*

DR ROSE    Still with me . . . ?
AMY    *(Garbled because his hands are in her mouth)* Aaargh . . .

DR ROSE   (*Hums along as the drilling gets louder*) You've heard his Goldberg reissue, haven't you?

AMY   Aaargh...

DR ROSE   (*Groans with pleasure*) Unbelievable!

*The drilling gets ferocious*

AMY   *Ow... ow!*

DR ROSE   Woops, sorry about that. Okay, you can rinse.

*Lights up on* AMY *lying prone in a dentist's chair with a bib around her neck. She rises up, takes a swig of water, sloshes it around in her mouth, and spits it emphatically into the little bowl next to her. She flops back down, wiping her mouth. She's in her forties.* DR ROSE *is several years older and on the dishevelled side.*

DR ROSE   Glenn Gould. Glenn Gould is the penultimate Bach keyboard artist of this century, period! Open, please. (*He resumes drilling*) No one else can touch him!

AMY   Aarg...

DR ROSE   Wanda Landowska, Roselyn Turek, Trevor Pinnock...forget it!

AMY   Aarg...

DR ROSE   (*Drilling with rising intensity*) Andras Schiff, Igor Kipness, Anthony Newman...no contest!

AMY   Aarg...

DR ROSE   Listen to the man...! The elegance of his phrasing, the clarity of his touch...The joy! The Joy! (*He roars*)

AMY   (*Practically jumping out of her seat*) Ooooowwwwwww!

DR ROSE   Sorry, sorry, afraid I slipped. (*His drilling returns to normal*) Hear how he hums along in a different key? The man can't contain himself.... (*He roars again, then calms down for a spate of drilling. He idly starts humming along with Gould*) You know, you're my third patient...no, make that fourth...that's pulled out a filling with candy this week. What was the culprit again?

AMY   (*Garbled*) Bit O'Honey.

DR ROSE   Almond Roca . . . ?

AMY   (*Garbled*) Bit O'Honey.

DR ROSE   Jujubes?

AMY   (*Less garbled*) Bit O'Honey, Bit O'Honey!

DR ROSE   Yup, saltwater taffy will do it every time! Okay, Amy, the worst is over. You can rinse. (*He hangs up the drill.* AMY *rinses and spits with even more fury*)

DR ROSE   Hey, hey, don't break my bowl on me! (*Fussing with his tools*) Now, where did I put that probe . . . ? I can't seem to hold on to anything these days . . . (AMY *flops back down with a sigh*)

DR ROSE   (*In a little singsong*) Where are you? . . . Where are you . . . ? Ahhhhh, here it is! Okay . . . let's just take one more last look before we fill you up. Open. (*He disappears into her mouth with the probe*) Amy, Amy, you're still grinding your teeth at night, aren't you!

AMY   (*Anguished*) Aaaaarrrrrrrhhh!

DR ROSE   You've got to wear that rubber guard I gave you!

AMY   (*Completely garbled*) But I can't breathe when it's on!

AMY   (*Incomprehensible*) I feel like I'm choking! I've tried to wear it, I really have, I just always wake up gasping for air. See, I can't breathe through my nose. If I could breathe through my nose, it wouldn't be a problem . . .

DR ROSE   I know they take getting used to, but you're doing irreparable damage to your supporting bone layer, and once that goes . . . (*He whistles her fate*)

*A* RADIO ANNOUNCER *has come on in the background during this*

RADIO ANNOUNCER  That was Glenn Gould playing Bach's Toccata in C minor, BWV listing 911. And to continue with our birthday tribute to J. S. Bach, we now turn to his Cantata BWV 80, 'Ein Feste Burg', as performed by the English Chamber Orchestra under the direction of Raymond Leppard. (*It begins*)

DR ROSE  (*Comes out of her mouth*) Well, let's whip up a temporary filling and get you out of here. (*He rummages through his tray of tools*)

AMY  Dr Rose, could I ask you something?

DR ROSE  Of course, today's March twenty-first, Bach's birthday! (*Some instruments fall; he quickly recovers them*) Woops...

AMY  I keep having this recurring nightmare.

DR ROSE  Oh, I love this piece. I used to sing it in college. Mind if I turn it up?

AMY  I just wonder if you've heard it before.

DR ROSE  (*Turns up the volume, singing along. He returns to his tray and starts sorting out his things, which keep dropping. He quickly retrieves them, never stopping his singing*)
*'Ein feste Burg ist unser Gott,*
*Ein gute Wehr und Waffen...* woops.
*Er hilft uns frei aus aller,* Not,
*Die uns itzt hat...* woops... *betroffen.'*

AMY  I have it at least three times a week now.

DR ROSE  I came this close to being a music major. *This* close!

AMY  I wake up exhausted with my whole jaw throbbing. Waa...waa...waa!

DR ROSE  Okay, let's just open this little bottle of cement here. (*He starts struggling with the lid*)

AMY  You know, the old . . . *teeth-granulating-on-you dream!* (*She stifles a sob*) You're at a party flashing a perfect smile when suddenly you hear this splintering sound like someone smashing teacups in the next room. . . ping . . . tock . . . crackkkkkkkkkk . . . tinkle, tinkle, 'Well, someone's having a good time!' you say to yourself, expecting to see some maniac swinging a sledgehammer. . . .

*Having a worse and worse time with the bottle,* DR ROSE *moves behind her chair so she can't see him*

DR ROSE  Ugh . . . ugh . . . ugh . . . ugh . . . ugh!

AMY  So you casually look around, and of course there *is* no maniac . . . ! Then you feel these prickly shards clinging to your lips. . . . You try and brush them away, but suddenly your mouth is filled with them. You can't spit them out fast enough! (*She tries*)

DR ROSE  *Goddamnit!* (*He goes through a series of silent contortions trying to open it – behind his back, up over his head, down between his legs, etc. etc.*)

AMY  (*Still spitting and wiping*) People are starting to stare . . . You try to save face. (*To the imagined party-goers*) 'Well, what do you know. . . . I seem to have taken a bite out of my coffee cup! Silly me!' (*She laughs, frantically wiping*)

DR ROSE  *Goddamn son of a bitch, what's going on here?*

AMY  That's just what *I* want to know!

DR ROSE  *Is this some kind of conspiracy or what?*

AMY  Why me? What did I do?

DR ROSE  They must weld these tops on.

AMY  Then I catch a glimpse of myself in the mirror . . .

DR ROSE  (*Starting to cackle*) Think you can outsmart me . . . ? (*He starts whacking a heavy tool down on the lid*)

AMY  You got it! My teeth are spilling out of my mouth in little pieces. I frantically try and moosh them back in, but there's nothing to hold on to. Then they start granulating on me ... fsssssssssssssss ... It's like trying to build a sand castle inside an hourglass!

DR ROSE *is having a worse and worse time. He finally just sits on the floor and bangs the bottle down as hard as he can, again and again.*

AMY  My mouth is a blaze of gums. We are talking pink for *miles* ...! Magellan staring out over the Pacific Ocean during a sunset in 1520 – (*As Magellan*) 'Pink ... pink ... pink!' (DR ROSE *starts to whimper as he pounds*)

AMY  What does it *mean*, is what I'd like to know! I mean, teeth are supposed to last forever, right? They hold up through floods, fires, earthquakes, and wars ... the one part of us that endures.

DR ROSE  Open, damnit. Open, damnit. Open, damnit ...

AMY  So if they granulate on you, where does that leave you? *Nowhere!*

DR ROSE  (*Curls into the foetal position and focuses on smaller moves in a tiny voice*) Come on ... come on ... Please? Pretty please? Pretty, lovely, ravishing please?

AMY  You could have been rain or wind, for all anybody knows. That's pretty scary ... (*Starting to get weepy*) One minute you're laughing at a party and the next you've evaporated into thin air ... (*Putting on a voice*) 'Remember Amy? Gee, I wonder whatever happened to her?' (*In another voice*) 'Gosh, it's suddenly gotten awfully chilly in here. Where's that *wind* coming from?' (*Teary again*) I mean, we're not around for that long as it is, so then to suddenly ... I'm sorry, I'm sorry. It's just I have this um ... long-standing ... Oh, God, here we go ... (*Starting to break down*) Control yourself! Control ... control!

DR ROSE *is now rolled up in a ball beyond speech. He clutches the bottle, whimpering and emitting strange little sobs.*

AMY See, I have this long-standing um...fear of death? It's something you're born with. I used to sob in my father's arms when I was only... Oh, boy! See, once you start thinking about it, I mean... *really* thinking about it... You know, time going on for ever and ever and ever and ever and you're not there.... It can get pretty scary...! We're not talking missing out on a few measly centuries here, but all... time! You know, dinosaurs, camel trains, cities, holy wars, boom! and back to dinosaurs again? (*More and more weepy*) Eternity!... Camel trains, cities, holy wars, boom! Dinosaurs, camel trains, cities, holy wars, boom!... Dinosaurs, camel trains, cities, holy wars.... Stop it Amy....just... *stop it!*

DR ROSE (*Broken*) I can't open this bottle.

AMY (*Wiping away her tears*) Dr Rose! What are you doing down there?

DR ROSE I've tried everything.

AMY What's wrong?

DR ROSE (*Reaching the bottle up to her*) I can't open it.

AMY (*Taking it*) Oh, here, let me try.

DR ROSE I'm afraid I'm having a breakdown.

AMY I'm good at this kind of thing.

DR ROSE I don't know, for some time now I just haven't...

AMY (*Puts the bottle in her mouth, clamps down on it with her back teeth, and unscrews the lid with one turn. She hands it back to him*) Here you go.

DR ROSE (*Rises and advances toward her menacingly*) You should never... *Never do that!*

AMY (*Drawing back*) What?

DR ROSE Open a bottle with your teeth.

AMY   I do it all the time.

DR ROSE   Teeth are very fragile. They're not meant to be used as tools!

AMY   Sorry, sorry.

DR ROSE   I just don't believe the way people mistreat them. We're only given one set of permanent teeth in a lifetime. *One set and that's it!*

AMY   I won't do it again. I promise.

DR ROSE   Species flourish and disappear, only our teeth remain. Open, please. (*He puts cotton wadding in her mouth*) You must respect them, take care of them... Oh, why even bother talking about it; no one ever listens to me, anyway. Wider, please. (*He puts in more cotton and a bubbling saliva drain*) Okay, let's fill this baby and get you on your way. (*He dabs in bits of compound*) So, how's work these days?

AMY   Aarg...

DR ROSE   Same old rat race, huh?

AMY   Aarg...

*During this, the final chorus, 'Das Wort sie sollen lassen stahn' has started to play*

AMY   (*Slightly garbled*) What is that tune? It's so familiar.

DR ROSE   'A Mighty Fortress Is Our God.'

AMY   Right, right! I used to sing it in Sunday school a hundred years ago.

DR ROSE   Actually, Bach stole the melody from Martin Luther.

AMY   (*Bursts into song, garbled, the saliva drain bubbling*) 'A Mighty Fortress Is Our God...'

AMY   . . . a bulwark never
    failing . . .
Our helper he amid
    the flood
Of mortal ills
    prevailing.
For still our ancient foe,
Doth seek to work us
    woe . . .

DR ROSE   (*Joining her*)
    *. . . Und kein' Dank dazu*
      *haben,*
*Er ist bei uns wehl auf*
    *dem Plan*
*Mit seinem Geist und*
    *Gaben.*
*Nehmen sie uns den Leib,*
*Gut, Ehr, Kind und*
    *Weib. . . .*

*Their voices swell louder and louder*

*Blackout*

# The Virtuous Burglar

**by Dario Fo**

**Farce** has to be funny to be deemed a success. It takes a combination of situations – for example various characters unexpectedly arriving at the same place – and pushes the possibilities of such coincidences to their limits. The most ferocious farces, such as those by Dario Fo and Joe Orton, have a dark undercurrent, showing us how fragile our world of order and polite conventions can be. In farce, everything threatens to fall apart. In this play the comic potential of the various encounters and coincidences quickly develops a momentum of its own.

## Characters

BURGLAR  *Daud*
BURGLAR'S WIFE  *Anita* .
MAN  *Daniel*
WOMAN  *Sarah*  ,
ANNA  *Chaurio* .
ANTONIO  *Franz*
SECOND BURGLAR  *Joe*  .

*A* BURGLAR, *having forced open a window, is climbing into a third-floor apartment in a well-to-do block of flats. On one side stands a classical shaded lamp. He looks around carefully. From the dark, we see furniture, rugs, old valuable paintings emerge. The* BURGLAR *closes the shutters, then switches on the light.*

*Just when he is about to pull open a drawer, the telephone rings. His first panic-stricken impulse is to make off as quickly as possible but then, realising that no one in the house comes to answer it and that he has nothing to fear, he returns to where he was. He would like to ignore the ringing of the phone but cannot. He makes his way stealthily over to the phone and leaps at it. He grabs the receiver and, almost as if he wished to suffocate it, presses it against his chest, covering it with his jacket. As though to make the act seem more criminal, an increasingly feeble and suffocated sound begins to emerge from the receiver.*

BURGLAR'S WIFE   Hello. Hello. Would you kindly answer... Who's speaking?

*The* BURGLAR *can finally let out a sigh of relief. The voice has stopped. The* BURGLAR *takes the receiver from under his jacket, raises it cautiously and puts it to his ear. Then he shakes it several times and hears a kind of groan.*

BURGLAR   Oh! At last.

BURGLAR'S WIFE   Ooooh! At last... who's speaking?

BURGLAR   (*Surprised once again*) Maria. Is that you?

BURGLAR'S WIFE   Yes, it's me. Why didn't you reply?

*At this point, lit up by one of the footlights, the figure of the woman who is speaking on the phone appears on the side of the stage which has so far remained in darkness.*

BURGLAR   You're crazy! Are you even phoning me at work now? Suppose there had been someone in the house. You're a great help you are.

BURGLAR'S WIFE   But you told me yourself that the owners were at their country cottage... anyway, I'm sorry, but I just couldn't stand it any more... I was worried about you... I didn't feel well... even a few moments ago, when I was ringing up, I could hardly breathe.

BURGLAR  Oh well, I'm sorry too, I didn't mean it, it never occurred to me that it might be you . . .

BURGLAR'S WIFE  And just what do you mean by that?

BURGLAR  Nothing, nothing . . . but let me get on . . . I've already wasted enough time.

BURGLAR'S WIFE  Ah, I'm wasting your time now! Thank you very much. Here I am in agony, nearly sick with worry . . . I don't know what to do with myself . . .

BURGLAR  What are you doing?

BURGLAR'S WIFE  I'm going through absolute hell, all because of you . . . and you treat me like this . . . charming, just charming that is . . . but don't worry . . . from now on I'm not interested . . . from now on don't even bother telling me where you're going, because as far as I am concerned . . .

BURGLAR  My dear, try and be reasonable . . . Can't you get it into your sweet head that I am not here for fun . . . just this once, couldn't you let me get on with my burgling in peace?

BURGLAR'S WIFE  There you go. You're at it again. Playing the martyr. There are plenty of people who burgle, shoplift, even go in for armed robbery without all this fuss. Just as well you stick to petty crime, otherwise God knows what sort of state I'd be in.

BURGLAR  (*Who has heard a strange noise behind him, instinctively putting his hand over the mouthpiece*) Quiet!

*Fortunately it was only the sound of the grandfather clock about to strike. It strikes midnight.*

BURGLAR'S WIFE  What's that?

BURGLAR  (*Recovering from his fright*) It's only the grandfather clock, thank goodness.

BURGLAR'S WIFE   What a clear sound it has! – It must be quite old. Is it very heavy?

BURGLAR   (*Absent-mindedly*) ... Might   be   quite ... (*Suddenly realising his wife's intentions*) Come on ... You're not really expecting me to bring it home ... sometimes I wonder...

BURGLAR'S WIFE   Oh no, don't you bother your little head about me ...   How could you imagine that I'd ask anything like that ... a nice thought from you! ... You giving a little present to me! ... The very idea!

BURGLAR   You're mad, that's what you are ... If I try to carry off that box, you tell me where to put the silver-ware and anything else I find.

BURGLAR'S WIFE   In the box ...

BURGLAR   (*Sarcastically*) You wouldn't like me to bring home a fridge? There's a nice big one through there, with a freezer department.

BURGLAR'S WIFE   Don't raise your voice, please. You're not at home now.

BURGLAR   Sorry, I got carried away.

BURGLAR'S WIFE   Besides, you might be overheard, and you'd look singularly ill-mannered.

BURGLAR   I've already said I'm sorry.

BURGLAR'S WIFE   And anyway, I didn't say I wanted a fridge, never mind one with a freezer compartment, I wouldn't know where to put it. But I would like a little something ... it's the thought that counts. I'll leave it to you. It's you that's giving the present, after all.

BURGLAR   How am I supposed to know what you would like. I've got other things on my mind right now.

BURGLAR'S WIFE   If that's all it is, I could come along and choose it myself.

BURGLAR   That's all I'd need!

BURGLAR'S WIFE   I'd love to see what a real luxury flat is

like. I'd make them die with envy at the coffee morning.

BURGLAR   It's me that'll die from something or other, not the women at the coffee morning . . . I'm here to burgle this house, can you not understand that? Cheerio, see you later.

BURGLAR'S WIFE   What's the rush? Is it too much for you to be nice to me once in a while? I am your wife after all. You even married me in church, not in a registry, like some whore, so you can't get out of it.

BURGLAR   (*Annoyed*) I've already said goodbye.

BURGLAR'S WIFE   Just a little kiss.

BURGLAR   Oh all right.

*He purses his lips in a comic way and emits a loud kissing sound*

BURGLAR'S WIFE   Do you love me?

BURGLAR   Yes, I love you.

BURGLAR'S WIFE   Very much?

BURGLAR   (*At the end of his tether*) Very, very much. But now will you put down the phone?

BURGLAR'S WIFE   You first.

BURGLAR   All right . . . me first.

*He is about to put the phone down when he hears his wife's voice assailing him loudly for the last time*

BURGLAR'S WIFE   Don't forget the present!

*The* BURGLAR *replaces the phone, staring at it all the while with hatred. At that moment the figure of the woman disappears in the dark. Finally alone, the* BURGLAR *begins to look around the apartment in search of his booty. He opens a drawer. He has clearly found the right one. He pulls a bag out of his jacket pocket and is about to start filling it when the sound of someone fumbling with the door lock makes him start. Voices are heard just offstage.*

WOMAN'S VOICE   There's a light in the living room. My God, I'm so frightened. Let's get out of here.

MAN'S VOICE   Calm down. I must have left it on myself. Who else do you imagine it might have been?

WOMAN'S VOICE   Suppose your wife has come back?

*Meantime the* BURGLAR, *in a state of terror, has attempted to climb out of the window but has lost too much time, so has no option but to dive inside the grandfather clock*

MAN   (*Entering cautiously*) What do you mean . . . my wife? What could have brought her back to town? (*Peering into every corner*) She wouldn't come even if she knew they were stripping the place. Well, are you satisfied? There's no one here.

WOMAN   (*Still cautious and suspicious*) I feel so guilty. (*As the* MAN *helps her off with her fur coat*) I wonder what you really think of me. Maybe I was wrong to give in to you so soon. I'm sure your wife resisted for much longer than me.

MAN   What's my wife got to do with it? She was always full of complexes, she had so many petty bourgeois prejudices . . . She wouldn't do it, just so she could get married in white.

WOMAN   (*Petulantly*) Yes, petty bourgeois, full of prejudices, but you married her just the same. I'd like to see if you would do the same for me.

MAN   (*Caressing her and trying to push her towards the centre-stage settee*) My dear . . . I assure you that if my wife didn't have so many old-fashioned ideas and if your husband were not so hostile . . . come closer to me.

*The* WOMAN *has sat down and the* MAN *moves closer to her*

WOMAN   (*Freeing herself from his embrace*) There, you have ruined everything. (*The* MAN *loses his balance and knocks against the back of the settee, which gives way. He ends up lying full length against the cushions*) Why did you have to remind me that I have a husband? What am I supposed to do now? You've brought back all my remorse, my guilt complex, my...

MAN   I'm sorry, I really didn't mean to. (*He gets up and replaces the settee back*) Maybe if we could talk about something else, just have a little chat, perhaps you'd manage to forget once again and we could go in there.

WOMAN   In where?

MAN   (*Awkwardly*) My bedroom.

WOMAN   Perhaps that is the best idea. Let's try.

MAN   (*Hopefully*) Try and go into my bedroom?

WOMAN   No. Try and chat a little.

MAN   Couldn't we go in there and chat?

WOMAN   Please, don't rush me. Let's just have a conversation, let's talk about when you were a child. I'm very fond of children.

MAN   (*Resigned*) Okay. If you don't mind. I'll begin from when I was five, because I don't remember anything before that.

WOMAN   Five! Pity, I prefer little children, they are more innocent, there's no harm in them...But if it's the best you can do...

MAN   Here we go. I remember that at five years old I was still a child, but I used to be taken for a six-year-old...(*Bursting out, irritated*) Oh no! For goodness' sake, enough of this. I feel a right idiot. You've been making a fool of me for a whole hour. First it was my wife, then your husband. Poor bastard, if he'd to put up with all this stopping and starting...

WOMAN   Not at all, it was quite different with him. He yielded right away.

MAN   (*Surprised*) What do you mean 'yielded right away'?

WOMAN  Just what I say. In his case, it was me who invited him up to my place, so it was up to me to make him succumb. (*Pompously*) If we separate the pleasure of conquest from love, what's left? Regrettably my husband has always been lamentably spineless and he gave in at once; (*Pause*) so I despise him. But with you, I have a feeling it will be different. You are so resolute once you make up your mind. Go on, be resolute.

MAN  Yes, I am being resolute. I resolve that we go through there right now.

*The two are about to go out, in each other's arms, when the telephone rings. They stop in embarrassment, not knowing what to do.*

MAN  Who could that be?

WOMAN  Your wife?

MAN  No, no... My wife... Why should she be phoning? Who would she be ringing? Certainly not me. She believes I'm at my mother's. Anyway it doesn't sound like a long distance call. It must be one of those heavy breathers or someone who's got the wrong number. (*Taking her in his arms again*) Let's go through, it'll stop in a minute.

*But the ringing continues regardless*

WOMAN  Please, make it stop, it's driving me mad.

MAN  (*Moves towards the phone, picks up the receiver and shuts it in the drawer of the telephone table*) There you are. It won't bother us now. I've knocked it off the hook.

WOMAN  (*In despair*) Oh my God! What have you done? Now they're bound to know that you're at home. Who else could have removed the receiver?

MAN  (*Realising, with dismay, that she is right*) What a fool! You're right. And they might even have suspected that I'm not on my own. They'll think I'm trying to hide something terrible.

WOMAN Thank you very much. Why don't you come right out and tell me that you only want me for one thing? (*Bursting into tears*) Just as I was letting myself be convinced . . . serves me right.

MAN (*Doing his utmost to appear in command of himself*) My dear, don't misunderstand me. Don't let's lose control for goodness' sake . . . let's stay calm . . . after all, why should they imagine for one moment that it was me who picked up the receiver? It could have been anyone, it could have been . . .

*He does not know how to go on*

WOMAN (*Ironically*) Certainly, someone just passing by.

MAN (*Awkwardly, with no conviction*) Why not?

WOMAN (*In the same tone*) Someone passing through by the merest chance . . . a burglar for example.

MAN Yes, could be . . . (*Realising the absurdity*) What do you mean 'a burglar'? If they thought that, they'd call the police.

WOMAN Right, and who knows, maybe they've done that already. (*Terrified*) Oh God! they'll find us here together, they'll arrest us. (*In a near scream*) The police! I want to go home.

*So saying, she rushes towards the door, followed by the* MAN *who tries to hold her back. At the same time the terrified* BURGLAR *comes out of his hiding place.*

MAN No, don't go away. Calm down.

BURGLAR The police, that's all I bloody need. Where the hell do I go now?

MAN (*From outside the living room*) Wait. Act your age.

WOMAN I'm frightened. Let's get out; there's no time to lose.

MAN   All right. Let's go, but I suppose you'll want your fur coat.

WOMAN   Oh yes, my fur coat. I'm completely mixed up. What a mess.

*The* BURGLAR *in the meantime has been undecided whether to escape through the window or wait until the two have gone out, but hearing them return he darts back to his hiding place. As he climbs back into the body of the grandfather clock, he strikes his head against the pendulum with a deep, resonant 'Dong'.*

BURGLAR   They're coming back! Nothing else for it. Move over, pendulum, be a pal. Ouch my head!

WOMAN   (*Frightened*) What's that?

MAN   (*Smiling*) Nothing my dear. Just the grandfather clock. It struck one.

WOMAN   I'm sorry, I'm a bundle of nerves.

*The* MAN *has the fur coat in his hand and is about to help the* WOMAN *put it on. The* WOMAN *notices that the receiver is still off the hook.*

WOMAN   You're not so calm and collected yourself. Look, we were going to leave the phone off the hook.

*She replaces the receiver. No sooner has she said these words than the phone begins to ring again. The two stare at each other, once more overcome by terror. The* MAN *almost hypnotised by the sound, grabs the phone and very slowly raises it to his ear.*

MAN   (*With a strained voice*) Hello.

*As before the figure of the* BURGLAR'S WIFE *appears and at the same time her intensely irritated voice is heard*

BURGLAR'S WIFE   About time too, I've been trying to get through for a full hour. Are you going to tell me why you cut me off?

MAN   I'm sorry, who's speaking please?

*His lover puts her ear close to the receiver so that she too can hear*

BURGLAR'S WIFE   Oh that's lovely, now you don't even recognise your own wife's voice.

WOMAN   (*Nearly fainting*) Your wife! I knew it! Oh my God!

BURGLAR'S WIFE   Who's that with you? How could you! I distinctly heard a woman's voice. Who is it?

MAN   (*Turning to his lover*) Calm down my dear. There must be some mistake. I have no idea who's on the phone. I've never heard this voice before.

BURGLAR'S WIFE   But I have. There's no point in you trying to wriggle out. You brute, you swine, I've found you out at last! Now I understand why you didn't want me to come to that house. But you'll need to come here sometime and I'll be waiting . . .

*The* BURGLAR *looks out of his hiding place to follow the conversation, and hearing his* WIFE's *voice he cannot help being gravely concerned*

MAN   (*Speaking into telephone*) Look, there's been some mistake. You've got the wrong number. This is the Frazosi house.

BURGLAR'S WIFE   I know that fine. Frazosi, 47 Via Cenini, Flat number 3. Now stop playing the fool and don't try disguising your voice any more. You don't do it very well. You swine . . . after telling me you didn't want to be disturbed at your work!

MAN   Who said he was working?

BURGLAR'S WIFE   Some work right enough! Mucking about with other women! Traitor, phoney, cheat, liar! They always said that a liar is a thief . . . I mean a thief is a liar.

MAN   What do you mean? Thief, phoney, who do you think you're talking to?

BURGLAR'S WIFE   To my husband. Who else?

MAN   If your husband is a phoney thief, that's your business, but I am not your husband, but the husband of my wife, who's not here, thank God, otherwise...

WOMAN   We'd all be done for!

BURGLAR'S WIFE   First of all, my husband is not a phoney thief. He's real thief...

MAN   Congratulations, Madam.

BURGLAR'S WIFE   And if you are not my husband, what are you doing in that house?

MAN   My dear lady, this is my own house.

BURGLAR'S WIFE   Oh excellent. You're in your own house, with a woman who is not your wife... alone, at this time of night, after spreading the word that you were out of town.

WOMAN   We've been found out!

BURGLAR'S WIFE   So, just like my husband, you too are a traitor, a cheat, a liar and therefore a thief.

MAN   I don't give a damn for your husband. But I would be very grateful if you would tell me who said I would be out of town.

BURGLAR'S WIFE   My husband. He always tells me where he is going. He's been keeping you under observation for ten days.

MAN   What?

BURGLAR'S WIFE   Yes, he was waiting for the right moment.

MAN   He was waiting for what? Why on earth did your husband want to know...

WOMAN   (*Covering the receiver with her hand*) But don't you see? Your wife has had you followed by that woman's husband, who must be a private detective.

MAN   Ah. Now I understand. So your husband offers this splendid service.

BURGLAR'S WIFE  Well, he's only doing his job.

MAN  A marvellous job too, if you think it's respectable to do everything you can to make a wife leave her husband.

BURGLAR'S WIFE  My husband make a wife leave her own husband? Watch what you're saying!

MAN  Stop acting the goat. And don't let on that you know nothing about it. (*Changing tone*) My wife ... playing a dirty trick like that on me. (*Pompously*) There's no doubt that in this world mutual trust is dead and buried, fool that I was to have deceived myself. 'There are certain things my wife would never stoop to,' I said to myself. 'She is a real lady, of the kind they do not make any more, even if she is a bit on the simple side.' It was me that was simple.

BURGLAR'S WIFE  What are you getting at? Are you implying that your wife and my husband ...

MAN  What do you mean 'implying'? I couldn't be more certain. For God's sake, quit the clowning.

BURGLAR'S WIFE  All right, all right, where is my husband now?

MAN  How should I know, if you don't know yourself?

BURGLAR'S WIFE  I only know that less than one hour ago he was there in your house.

MAN  Here, in this house?

BURGLAR'S WIFE  Certainly, I phoned him myself. In fact I thought he was still there.

WOMAN  He must have got the keys from your wife.

MAN  Precisely, so that he could come and go at all hours of the day and night. I bet he's already down at the Villa Ponente.

BURGLAR'S WIFE  Villa Ponente. And why should my husband be down there?

MAN  (*Ironically*) Oh come on. Didn't he tell you? I

thought he never hid anything from you about what he was doing and where he was going. Anyway, just to keep you happy, here's the address. Villa Ponente, 34 Via Aristide Zamboni, telephone number 7845 ... My wife's there ... though she won't be my wife much longer.

*With these words, he puts down the phone in a temper. The other* WOMAN *bursts into bitter tears. The figure of the* BURGLAR'S WIFE *vanishes.*

WOMAN   What a scandal! I'll be disgraced. When my husband finds out, it'll be a terrible blow for him, poor thing. When I think of all the sacrifices I've made to keep him in the dark ... to hide even the tiniest details from him ... so as not to upset him ... even this most recent affair ... and now, caught in the act ...

MAN   And do you not think it's worse for me? I had just made up my mind to retire from the town council, but now, after this scandal, they'll put me up for mayor.

WOMAN   Well, what can we do? We can either run away or give ourselves up.

MAN   There's no need to go over the score, give ourselves up! To whom, may I ask? And what for? What are we supposed to have done after all? It's not as though they caught us red-handed. No, we were just having a chat ... we were talking about children ...

WOMAN   That's true enough. I was just telling you how much I liked children.

MAN   Exactly. But perhaps it would be better not to mention that. People can be very evil-minded. They would accuse us of premeditation. What an outrage. I'd shoot myself.

WOMAN   What a good idea! Perhaps that's the best way out, the only real solution.

MAN   What? The only solution! Are you mad? I can just see the headlines! 'Local Councillor, after presiding at over fifty civil weddings shoots himself for adultery.' They'd laugh their heads off at the town hall!

WOMAN   I am glad you find it all so funny... sometimes I wonder about you... you've no sense of responsibility.

MAN   Why should I blame myself? We're in a trap and there's nothing for it but to wait an hour or two until my wife arrives from Villa Ponente. (*Thinking it over*) An hour or two? Why not make full use of it? At least they'll have something to sentence us for. (*He goes towards the* WOMAN *who is still seated on the sofa*) Let's go in there now.

WOMAN   Don't be so vulgar, please.

*She pushes the* MAN, *who ends up in the same position as previously, full length on the settee with his head over the back which has again given way*

MAN   (*Cursing, striking his open hand against the settee*) And I bought the bloody thing myself!

WOMAN   Is it asking too much for you to show even the tiniest bit of concern... of understanding for me? Don't you understand that I am in despair?

MAN   You always exaggerate! 'In despair.' Would you be kind enough to tell me what you want of me. (*With a theatrical pose*) Do you want me to shoot myself? All right then, I'll shoot myself. I keep a little pistol handy for emergencies. (*The* MAN *takes a pistol from a drawer and aims it at his forehead*) Maybe now you'll be happy.

WOMAN   Nooooo! What are you doing? Stop it. Give me that.

*She takes the gun from his hand while the* MAN, *who has obviously made the gesture only to frighten her, laughs quietly*

MAN (*Ironic but satisfied*) What? Now you don't want me to shoot myself?

WOMAN My dear, you'll have to take off the safety catch and put a bullet in the gun. Like that. (*She snaps the loaded gun together and hands it back to him*) There you are. Now you can shoot yourself.

MAN (*With a strangely squeaky voice*) Ha . . . Ha . . . Now I can . . .

WOMAN (*Raising the gun until it is level with his face*) Come on, hurry up. You don't want to be still alive when your wife gets here now do you . . .

*The* MAN, *petrified, puts the gun against his forehead and just at that moment the grandfather clock strikes twelve-thirty. At the first sounds, the* MAN *starts back and stares at the gun in terror.*

WOMAN What a funny clock, first it strikes one, and then it strikes midnight . . . seems to be going slow . . . I mean going backwards.

MAN It certainly is strange . . . that never happened before . . . perhaps it's a sign from heaven. The hand of destiny that comes to arrest the suicide's hand . . . to remind him that time, that life can be ended but that no traveller returns from that undiscovered bourne. Oh my grateful thanks to you, blessed heavenly hand! My darling grandfather clock you have saved my life!

*With these words, he goes up to the clock, embraces it warmly as if it were a person in flesh and blood. The clock goes on striking and seems to spring to life.*

BURGLAR'S VOICE (*Obviously unable to hold back cries of pain caused by the pendulum striking his head*) Ouch . . . Oh . . . damnation . . . stop.

MAN (*Leaping backwards and going over to embrace the* WOMAN *who is now rigid with fear*) Destiny!!

BURGLAR (*Comes out massaging his head*) Oooh, the pain! – that was sore! Good evening. If you don't mind, could you let me have some soda water? I'm coming up in huge lumps all over.

WOMAN (*Scandalised*) Lumps! A bit vulgar for Destiny!

MAN Who in the name of God are you? What are you doing in my house? Answer, or else I'll give you a sight more than lumps.

WOMAN Please, don't you start being rude as well. After all, what harm can it do to give him a drop of soda water?

BURGLAR Come on, just a teensy weensy glass of soda water, after all...

MAN (*Very decisively, pointing the gun at him*) Don't make me lose my patience. Who are you? Who are you?

BURGLAR (*Terrified*) There's no need to be pointing that at me. I'll tell you right away sir...I am the husband...you see, that woman who phoned a while ago, she's my wife...and I'm her husband.

MAN Ah...You're the husband...good.

BURGLAR Yes. We got married in church.

MAN I'm pleased to hear it. So you'll have the good fortune to be buried in consecrated ground.

BURGLAR Buried! No, No, No. You can't get rid of me like that. (*Turning to the* WOMAN) You've no right. Madam, you're a witness that I am unarmed. You'd better watch out. Anyone who shoots me will catch it, and no mistake. Paragraph 127 of the Criminal Justice Act. You can, at the most, fire in the air if I attempt to escape. But since I'm not escaping, you can't. I warn you that the charge would be first degree murder.

WOMAN You people are always well up on the law...of

course the law is always on your side. But suppose we just decided to shoot you in the back, as they do with spies. (*Turning to the* MAN) That's what to do. Shoot him in the back. (*To the* BURGLAR) Kindly turn round.

BURGLAR  I'm awfully sorry, but I really don't like war games. Why don't we just call the police?

MAN  Ah! He's smart, this one. Call the police! The police uncover the adultery, we're sent packing and he carries off the reward.

BURGLAR  A reward! Me? From whom?

MAN  From my wife.

BURGLAR  You're out of your mind. I've no idea who your wife is.

WOMAN  What a hypocrite. You don't know her! Shoot him at once, please, he's getting on my nerves.

MAN  Just a moment. How long were you in there?

*Pointing to the clock*

BURGLAR  From precisely 13 minutes to twelve. I went in just as you arrived. Why?

MAN  So if he was inside the clock, he can't have phoned yet. If we get a move on, we might still be safe.

WOMAN  Yes, safe, with him there ready to blow the whistle on us.

BURGLAR  (*Without understanding what they are talking about, willing to do anything to remove the danger*) No! Me blow a whistle! I don't know how to blow a whistle. I never learned, strike me down dead if I tell a lie. (*He blows into the barrel of the gun, which is only a few inches from his mouth, as if it were a whistle*) You see?

MAN  Besides, if we killed him, it would be a bit too obvious.

WOMAN  Suppose we just gave him a really serious wound.

MAN   What good would that do?

BURGLAR   I couldn't agree more. What good would it do?

WOMAN   I know what good it would do. If you could get him on one particular nerve. (*She touches him at the back of the neck*) For example in the neck, this one which passes right behind here, between the atlas and the epistropheus. He would lose his memory completely.

MAN   Are you sure?

WOMAN   Positive. In any case, he'd be completely paralysed, he wouldn't be able to speak and from our point of view that would be just as good.

BURGLAR   (*Who already feels paralysed*) But not for me it wouldn't. Is there not some other way, a little less risky? Come on lady, think up another idea. You've got brains.

WOMAN   (*Flattered*) Yes, there might be another solution: get him drunk. No one would believe the evidence of a drunk.

MAN   That's true. I've always thought you were marvellous.

BURGLAR   (*With a sigh of relief*) Absolutely marvellous. I knew it as soon as I saw you. (*Rubbing his hands*) Well, what have you got to drink? If it's all the same with you, I'd rather have red wine. White wine gives me indigestion. Ever since I was a boy...

MAN   No, not wine, it takes too long. It's far better with gin or whisky. Three good glasses should do the trick.

BURGLAR   Well...whisky doesn't really agree with me. It smells of oil.

WOMAN   (*Who in the meantime has filled a glass to the brim*) There's no oily smell with this one. It's genuine Scotch whisky.

MAN   What's it like?

BURGLAR   (*Savouring it like a real connoisseur*) Very good indeed! Quite excellent.

MAN   (*Drinking in turn*) It damn well ought to be. It cost me a packet.

BURGLAR   (*Pretentiously*) Could I have another soupçon?

MAN   (*To the* BURGLAR *who holds out his glass to have it filled up again*) Take it easy. If you swallow the lot, what are we supposed to have?

WOMAN   Where are your manners? Anyway, it's him who is supposed to be getting drunk isn't it?

BURGLAR   Yes, it's me. (*Becoming bolder*) But if you want, why don't you get sozzled as well? Ha, Ha, Ha, wait till my wife hears about this. She'll never believe it. (*The thought of his wife wipes the smile from his face*) Talking of my wife, what did you tell her to drive her into such a temper? You've landed me right in it. You two go and phone her right away and explain your little ploy to her.

MAN   Ploy? What ploy?

BURGLAR   You know. That you're getting me drunk to stop me talking... about whatever it is that's bothering you.

WOMAN   Do you hear that? He wants a witness, the villain. You were right all along. Better to shoot him at once, and get it over with.

MAN   Yes, much better. (*He goes to get the gun which he has left in the drinks cupboard, but the* BURGLAR *gets there first, seizes the gun and aims it at the* MAN) Now none of this nonsense! That's my gun! Give it back to me this minute.

BURGLAR   It's all change now. First you keep me locked up in that tomb getting knocked about by the pendulum, then you set my wife against me, then you want to paralyse me with my epistropheus. Time to stop fooling about. I came here to burgle, not to play the clown.

MAN   To burgle!

BURGLAR   Indeed. I'm a burglar. The real thing.

WOMAN   (*Amused*) A burglar. Now it all comes out. I've never heard such nonsense. Where's your black mask, your striped jersey, your felt shoes?

MAN   Exactly. Where are they?

BURGLAR   Black mask! Felt shoes! This isn't a cartoon in one of your colour supps. Anyway what do you know about burglars and robbers?

WOMAN   (*Pompously*) For your instruction, I know everything there is to know about robbers, thieves, swindlers, burglars etc. I was on a TV quiz show. My subject was 'Celebrated Crimes and Thefts'.

MAN   Oh now I see where all your knowledge about the use and care of guns comes from. (*To the* BURGLAR) I'm sorry...bad luck...choose another profession. This just won't do at all.

BURGLAR   Listen you, have you ever heard of the Martello gang?

WOMAN   (*In the tone of someone repeating by heart*) The Martello Gang, leading members Mangia, Serafini, and Angelo Tornati nicknamed Stanca.

BURGLAR   Angelo Tornati nicknamed Stanga, with a g. It's a dialect word meaning long.

WOMAN   Long...don't be absurd...he's just a little fellow.

MAN   (*Just to say something*) You mean 'smallish'.

BURGLAR   Why, do I seem smallish to you?

MAN   What have you got to do with it?

BURGLAR   What have I got to do with it? Allow me to introduce myself. I am Angelo Tornati, nicknamed Stanga. And if you don't believe it, here are my release papers from St Stephen's Prison. (*He pulls out some documents*) I did three years.

WOMAN  (*A smile spreading over her face after glancing at the papers*) Wonderful! It really is him. Stanca, sorry Stanga. Marvellous. May I? (*She embraces him, kisses him on the cheek*) A robber, a real robber... I've never met a real robber before... let me have a look at you.

MAN  (*Jealous*) What are you up to now? This scoundrel comes to burgle my house... and you kiss him... it's disgusting.

WOMAN  Watch your language! 'It's disgusting.' What do you know about it? Have you ever kissed a robber?

MAN  No.

WOMAN  Well then. You try, and then tell me if it's quite as disgusting as you say.

*At that moment the doorbell rings*

WOMAN  Who can that be?

BURGLAR  I bet it's my wife again. (*Lifting the phone*) Perhaps now you'll be good enough to explain to her. Hello Maria. You've landed me in a right fix with your telephone calls. I've told you time and again that when I'm at work you must leave me in peace. You must not disturb me, even if the house goes on fire. I want you to stay at home and not bother about anything.

MAN  It's not the phone... it's the doorbell.

BURGLAR  (*Looking at the phone with annoyance*) So that's why she let me talk.

*He hangs up*

MAN  (*Opens the window and looks out*) Who is it?

WOMAN'S VOICE  Who do you think? It's me, Anna.

WOMAN  (*Turning pale*) Oh God... this time it really is his wife.

MAN (*Trying to sound perfectly natural*) Ah it's you, dear. I wasn't expecting you. What's happened?

ANNA That's what I wanted to ask you. I had some mad female on the phone shouting insults.

BURGLAR A mad female! That's my wife. I might have known.

ANNA Why don't you open the door? What's keeping you?

MAN Just coming . . . (*Moving away from the window*) Now we're for it. What do we tell her?

BURGLAR Bye, Bye, don't call me. I'll leave by the window.

MAN (*Grabbing him by the collar*) Oh no you don't. Very convenient. It's thanks to you and your wife that we're all in this mess, so it's up to you to get us out.

BURGLAR Me! What do you want me to do?

MAN (*Turning to the* WOMAN) Just a minute, if you two could pass yourselves off as man and wife . . . we'd be OK.

WOMAN What! Me married to him! We haven't even been introduced.

MAN Don't worry, love follows after. Anyway, it's always better to be taken for the wife of a phoney husband than the lover of a real husband. (*Preparing to go and meet his* WIFE) Right then, everybody ready. (*Picking up the gun*) I'll take this now , thank you. Remember, no fooling about, otherwise . . . (*Clicks the gun shut*) I don't want to have to use this.

WOMAN Oh my God, how dreadful. (*Looking the* BURGLAR *over from head to toe*) If you're going to be my husband, stand up, let me see you. Couldn't you have put on something neater? It's always the same, when we're visiting other people, you always make me so embarrassed . . . You know that when a man looks untidy, it's always the wife's fault.

BURGLAR  I know, I know but...I didn't exactly expect things to turn out like this. I've got a nice checked suit at home. I'll pop over and put it on, if you like.

WOMAN  No you won't. (*Looking at his bulging pockets*) Your pockets are stuffed with things.

BURGLAR  (*Straightening up like a tailor's dummy*) It's the latest style didn't you know?

ANNA  (*Voice heard coming from outside*) So what's all this? Who's here with you?

MAN  That's what I was trying to tell you. There's been a misunderstanding but now it's all cleared up.

ANNA  Misunderstanding? You can say that again. You were supposed to be at your mother's, but instead I find you here.

MAN  (*Entering, followed by* WIFE) I'm trying to explain. Here we are, this is my friend Doctor Angelo Tornato.

BURGLAR  (*Drily*) Tornati.

MAN  (*With a weak smile*) Sorry. And this is his wife.

BURGLAR  It was your husband who made us get married. Love follows after, so he told us.

MAN  (*Covering up*) In my official capacity, at the registry.

WOMAN  Please forgive this intrusion, I realise it's a bit late, not very convenient for you, but we had to turn to your husband, because...it so happened...well you see...

ANNA  (*Drily*) Never mind that. Was it you who telephoned me?

MAN  (*Intervening quickly*) Yes. It was her. But you must understand, the poor thing was so distraught.

WOMAN  Do forgive me, but I was nearly driven crazy by jealousy, I don't know why, but I had the idea that my husband was having an affair with you. But now that I see you, I don't know how I could have thought such a thing.

ANNA   Why, do I look as though I'm past it? Or do you want to come right out and say that I'm some kind of monster.

WOMAN   No, no I didn't mean that at all. You look very elegant. I meant, knowing the vulgar tastes of my husband as I do . . .

BURGLAR   Me! Vulgar tastes!

ANNA   I am sorry that you feel vulgar, my dear, since your husband married you, but that doesn't mean that you have to consider me low enough to end up with a man like your aforementioned spouse.

BURGLAR   That's quite enough, first vulgar, now low and aforementioned.

MAN   (*Evidently attempting to defuse the situation*) No need to overdo it, dear. He is not much to look at but he might be all right for some tastes!

ANNA   What a husband I have! Instead of being outraged when they cast aspersions on his own wife, he says that I might get to like my supposed lover. The man's mad!

WOMAN   No, your husband didn't mean that. He just meant that when a woman is in love, she always thinks that other women might like her husband no matter how vulgar his tastes are.

ANNA   That's lovely that is. You mean that because I'm fond of my husband, you must be fond of him as well, is that it? Seeing you are here, why don't you take him as your lover?

WOMAN   No thank you.

ANNA   (*Turning to* BURGLAR) And what do you say to all this?

BURGLAR   To be quite honest, I'd sooner have her as a lover than as a wife . . . always assuming your husband had nothing against it . . . it's all up to him. It was him who married us.

ANNA (*Bursting out laughing, in obvious good humour*) Very good, very witty. Now I see why your wife is afraid of other women. Witty men are the most dangerous. Especially if they have vulgar tastes.

BURGLAR (*To the* WOMAN) She called me vulgar again!

WOMAN (*Affectionately, putting her arm around him*) Ah yes, he really is dangerous. You've no idea.

MAN (*Annoyed*) You're overdoing it a bit. (*Correcting himself*) All men are dangerous, to some extent.

ANNA Certainly not you, my love! (*Looking at the* BURGLAR *and the* WOMAN *who are holding hands tenderly*) Aren't they lovely. They look like two newly-weds on honeymoon. You were made for each other . . . weren't they dear?

MAN (*Getting riled*) Yes, but now . . . it's time to be saying goodnight . . . it's getting late.

ANNA Where are your manners? Take no notice, just stay as long as you please. Why don't we all have a little drink?

BURGLAR Why not? The same whisky as before for me.

*He grabs the bottle but the* WOMAN *signals 'no' to him*

WOMAN (*Whispering*) Put that down! (*In a strained voice, to* ANNA) You're very kind, but we've already taken advantage of your courtesy . . . (*The* BURGLAR *puts the bottle in his pocket*) It really is late, and I wouldn't want my husband to come and (*Realising what she has said*) . . . I mean, him to get home too late . . . we live quite a way off, right at the other end of the town, and he must get up early tomorrow morning, isn't that right dear?

BURGLAR Eh?

ANNA   Well, why not stay the night? We've got a spare room. Go on, dear, you make them.

MAN   (*His mind elsewhere*) Yes, why not sleep here tonight. (*Realising what he has said*) What am I saying? Perhaps they prefer...

BURGLAR   Oh, we'd be quite happy.

ANNA   Good, you see. They'd rather stay here. I can't tell you how pleased I am.

WOMAN   (*Making a last effort*) But really... we've got nothing with us, and my husband can't sleep without his pyjamas.

ANNA   If that's all. (*To her* HUSBAND) You can give him your pyjamas, the ones you haven't worn yet, can't you?

MAN   (*In despair*) Yes!

ANNA   (*To the* WOMAN) Would you like to come with me and I'll show you the room. You'll be perfectly comfortable, I'm sure. (*To the* BURGLAR) I'll have to steal her from you for a moment.

*The two* WOMEN *go out. The two* MEN, *left alone, stare at each other, the one with embarrassment, the other with hatred. The first to speak is the owner of the house.*

MAN   Did you really have to go on like that? You're nothing but a half-witted Casanova... but if you think you're going to sleep with my... my... my pyjamas... you can get that idea out of your head right away.

BURGLAR   Whose idea was it in the first place? Who had the great idea of making me pretend to be the husband of your lady-friend? And then you go all of a twitter... A man who's never had a day's luck in his life comes here to earn his living ... not only do you stop him going off with as much as a broken alarm clock, but you make him take part in your cavortings!

No, no, I'm very sorry, but now you phone up my wife...No, a better idea, let's get your wife in here and we'll tell her everything...then I'll call the police. I'd sooner be interrogated by a police sergeant than by my wife.

MAN   Listen to that! An officer and a gentleman! I do believe he's offended. We disturbed him at his back-breaking work. You came here to burgle. All right, get on with it. Burgle away. (*He opens the silverware drawer*) There are some gold teaspoons there, help yourself.

BURGLAR   (*Takes out his bag, opens it but then thinks better of it*) No thank you, but stealing things in this way is not my style. Another time perhaps.

MAN   (*Who is beginning to get jumpy. He makes as though to take the gun from his pocket*) I have ways of making you. With this!

BURGLAR   If you really insist. (*He handles a spoon very delicately*) Yes, quite a pleasing little piece, this spoon.

*He sticks it into his jacket pocket*

MAN   (*Taking out his gun menacingly*) I told you to steal...so do it thoroughly. I don't want you to go around telling people there's nothing much to steal in my house...or complaining that we exploit burglars.

BURGLAR   I never said that.

MAN   You're just the type to say it. Come on, take these as well.

*He opens a drawer and hands him a bundle of silver spoons*

BURGLAR   I really don't want to abuse your kindness, your hospitality.

MAN   No need for scruples. Just get on with the job. I've got a gun, remember.

*At that very moment, the* BURGLAR'S WIFE *comes in, and seeing the* MAN *pointing a gun at her husband, lets out a piercing scream and throws herself between the two, clinging to her husband*

BURGLAR   Maria! How did you get here?

BURGLAR'S WIFE   The door was open.

BURGLAR   And I had to clamber three flights up a roan pipe to get here.

BURGLAR'S WIFE   Forgive me, it was all my fault, I know... I only understood too late... but now you'd better give everything back... even if they give you a few months, it's quite near the festive season and it's not too bad doing a stretch at this time of the year... they even give you Christmas cake and tangerines ... please give yourself up.

MAN   Not his wife, not her as well! What am I going to tell my wife when she finds out that he has two wives?

BURGLAR'S WIFE   Who has two wives?

BURGLAR   (*His voice high-pitched from terror*) I've nothing to do with this, remember. It was him that told me to take her as my wife in case his wife found out that she wasn't my wife... just a wife...

BURGLAR'S WIFE   Give me that gun. I'll teach him a lesson. (*Snatches the gun from the* MAN'S *hands and points it at her husband*) Ah ha! you wicked traitor, liar, villain... fool that I was to believe that you were getting along fine with your wife when you've had another wife all the time... and she's not even his wife... I'll kill you. (*Tries to remove the safety catch*) How does this thing work?

MAN   I'll show you. Oh God what am I doing? Never mind. (*Snatches the gun*) For God's sake don't make such a din. If the other two wives hear us, I'm done for and no mistake, but so's your husband. Listen to me one minute. I am not going to explain all the whys and wherefores, it would take too long, but if you want to save your husband, stay calm. (*Footsteps are heard, coming nearer*) Damn . . . here they are . . . what in God's name can we say now!

ANNA   (*Entering*) What a lovely woman you married, Signor Tornati . . . she's waiting for you . . . I've brought you down these pyjamas myself because if I were waiting for my husband . . . (*She stops, surprised at seeing the new guest whom the* BURGLAR *and her husband are trying to hide from her view*) . . . I have . . . Sorry dear . . . Who is this lady?

MAN   (*As if unaware of her existence*) Who?

BURGLAR'S WIFE   I'm a wife . . . Maria Tornati.

ANNA   What? Another wife?

MAN   (*Trying to redeem the situation*) Yes, I was just going to tell you . . . this lady claims to be . . .

BURGLAR'S WIFE   Claims to be! I am the wife.

MAN   Exactly, I am the wife . . . she is the wife. (*Staring hard at her, as if trying to hypnotise her*) The first wife of my friend Tornato.

BURGLAR   (*Correcting*) Ti.

MAN   (*Uncertain*) To – ti.

BURGLAR   Ti . . . ti . . . ti . . . Tornati.

MAN   The first wife from whom he is now divorced.

*The* BURGLAR'S WIFE *tries to interrupt, but her husband nudges her with his elbow*

ANNA   Are you foreigners?

BURGLAR   Eh . . . no, we are . . .

ANNA   Then how were you able to get divorced?

BURGLAR   (*Asking the* MAN *for help*) Eh? Able?

MAN   (*Turning to* BURGLAR'S WIFE) Able?

ANNA   Ah . . . I understand . . . your friend works in the cinema.

MAN   Yes, yes, yes, he works in the cinema. He's a film producer.

ANNA   A producer! And what kind of films does he make? (*Noticing the bag he has in his hand*) What's that in your hand? (*Opens the bag*) My best silver! What are you doing?

BURGLAR   A spot of burgling.

MAN   Noooo... he was telling me about the subject of a new film of his... where there is a scene involving a theft... and he was showing me...

ANNA   Oh how interesting. So you're a specialist.

BURGLAR   Yes, father and son...

ANNA   Your wife too?

BURGLAR'S WIFE   No... not me. My husband won't let me, he always leaves me at home.

ANNA   No, I meant... this business of the divorce... if they are divorced, how come his wife is still his wife... he seems to have two.

MAN   Precisely... He got divorced... then remarried... but then the State, over-riding Church Law, didn't recognise the divorce, even though it had earlier recognised, in civil law, the second marriage... so that the poor thing now finds himself at one and the same time a bigamist, an adulterer, a public sinner and a devout Catholic.

BURGLAR'S WIFE   What! (*To her husband*) You never said a word to me.

BURGLAR   I didn't know. (*To the house owner*) What do you mean, a devout bigamist?

*The* MAN *pushes him away from the women*

ANNA   (*To the* BURGLAR'S WIFE) Just as well for you. There are some things it's better not to know. Even when you do know them, you still don't understand. Poor thing! Who knows where it'll end. Maybe they'll put him on trial and send him to jail like a petty thief.

MAN   Maybe. Just like someone who makes off with the cutlery (*pointedly*) and all because he has a wife.

ANNA   What?

MAN   I mean two wives.

ANNA   (*To the* BURGLAR) Which reminds me, your other wife, shouldn't we let her know that she's here. (*Pointing to the* BURGLAR'S WIFE) What bad luck for her. I don't see what else we can do. Even if you all agreed, it's really just a one-and-a-half sized bed. You wouldn't be very comfortable.

MAN   Never mind ... we'll fix something up.

BURGLAR'S WIFE   You'd better ... you're not getting off that lightly.

BURGLAR   (*Would like to take the bag, but is obliged to leave it so as to push his* WIFE *towards the door on the left*) Yes, yes ... but let's get out now. Damn! I'll have to leave the takings.

MAN   (*To* BURGLAR'S WIFE) Don't go yet. Come in here and meet your husband's wife ... I mean ... this way.

BURGLAR   I'm coming too.

ANNA   (*Watches the three go out and shakes her head with compassion*) Poor woman! (*Then, seeing the bottles scattered on the table*) What a mess. They've certainly been drinking.

*She pours herself a drink. In the meantime a man appears at the door and calls quietly to her.*

ANTONIO   Anna ... are you alone?

ANNA   Oh my God! Antonio, are you out of your mind? Go away ... at once ... my husband's at home.

ANTONIO   What on earth's up? You were just not making any sense on the phone. What's all this about my wife phoning you?

ANNA   Nothing, nothing at all. It's all been a mistake, thank God! I had a phone call from a woman who insulted me because of her husband.

ANTONIO   And you thought it was my wife?

ANNA   Exactly, I don't know your wife, much less her voice but I got such a fright. Anyway, you can't stay here. Away you go. I'll see you tomorrow.

ANTONIO   Ah, you want me out of the way now. No, no, I'm not having that. What do you take me for? A telephone call, some funny misunderstanding, your husband coming home when he's supposed to be at his mother's . . . no, no, there's more to all this. You know what I think? I think it was all set up to cancel our date so that you could meet someone else here. Who it was I don't know, but certainly not your husband.

ANNA   You're mad. How can you think such a thing?

ANTONIO   Stop lying. What about these glasses. It's quite clear . . . you were preparing yourself, spiritually. Where is . . . what's his name? Speak, it'd be better for you. (*Seizing her by the shoulders*) Who is he?

*At that moment the* BURGLAR *appears with the pyjamas still under his arm. He's come back for the bag. But at the sight of this scene and of the new guest, he drops the bag in fright, at which* ANTONIO *turns round.*

BURGLAR   Don't let me disturb you. I'm just picking up my bag.

ANTONIO   Ah, here he is . . . with his pyjamas neatly rolled up . . . the young gentleman's ready and willing.

BURGLAR   (*To* ANTONIO *who has grabbed his arm*) Just lay off, the lady gave me these herself. You can have them if you like. There's no need to get all worked up over a pair of pyjamas.

ANTONIO  I know she gave them to you, don't I just! And now I'll make you both pay. (*With these words, he locks the door and puts the key in his pocket*) No one's leaving until you explain.

ANNA  Antonio...I beg you...you're making a terrible mistake...this man's a friend of my husband's and he's here as our guest with his wives...

*From the other rooms, the shouts of the two* WOMEN, *evidently quarrelling, can be heard*

VOICES OF THE TWO WOMEN  No, no I'm not the village idiot, you know...don't give me all that stuff, you little whore. (*Other voice*) Who are you calling a whore? Just mind your language.

ANTONIO  (*Releasing his grip*) So they really are your wives? How many have you got?

*The* BURGLAR *makes a gesture of his hands as though to say 'quite enough'*

ANNA  Please, please, please, Mr Tornati...don't breathe a word of this to my husband.

BURGLAR  No, no, not a word.

ANTONIO  That's very good of you. I'm sorry about this misunderstanding.

BURGLAR  What's one more misunderstanding among friends? What a night this has been!

ANNA  You must fly now. Where have you put the key?

ANTONIO  In my coat. (*He searches in his pocket*) Oh damn! It's slipped down into the lining. There's a hole in the pocket. Ooooh, what next? Don't just stand there. Give me a hand.

*He takes off his coat to make the search easier. All three take part in the operation to locate the key, which seems to have a life of its own and keeps eluding them.*

ANNA   Got it! No, you knocked it out of my hand.

BURGLAR   Stop. Here it is. Oh no, where's it got to now?

ANTONIO   Take it easy. You're ripping the lining apart. Hell, it's gone into the sleeves now.

*The voices from the adjoining room draw closer*

ANNA   Here, they're coming. Now what do we do?

BURGLAR   Come over here. I was in here for a couple of hours. (*Opens the grandfather clock*) You can make yourself quite comfortable. (*Pushing him in*) Just watch out when it starts striking ... You can get a right nasty one ... and no smoking!

*The two women come in, followed by the* MAN. *They are somewhat distraught.*

BURGLAR'S WIFE   (*To her* HUSBAND) Since these two are not going to tell me anything, let's go home and you can explain everything.

BURGLAR   Go home? What's the rush? We're all having such a wonderful time. What lovely people! Look, they've even given me a pair of pyjamas. Anyway, I don't know how on earth we're going to get out. There's no key.

BURGLAR'S WIFE   (*Shaking the door*) It shouldn't be very hard for you to pick the lock. That's your job isn't it.

*The* BURGLAR *takes an enormous bunch of keys out of his pocket*

BURGLAR   Would one of these do?

ANNA   (*To her husband*) What a lot of keys! What's he got all them for?

MAN   I told you, he's a film producer, and you show me a film producer that doesn't have at least five or six offices, two or three villas, and a couple of pied-à-terres.

*At that very moment, the grandfather clock begins to strike. First a blow, then a shout of pain and the unfortunate inhabitant of the clock comes out cursing.*

ANTONIO Ouch, that was sore...my poor head... ooooh.

BURGLAR I told you so! I told you you'd get it in the skull, and there's not even any soda water in this house.

WOMAN (*Panic-stricken*) It's my husband. (*Trying to appear nonchalant*) Hello dear.

ANTONIO Julia! What are you doing here?

ANNA What? You know Mr Tornati's wife?

ANTONIO Whose wife? You must be joking, Julia's my wife.

MAN (*Turning to his wife*) No, no, dear, don't worry. There's been a misunderstanding.

BURGLAR Another one! What a lot of misunderstandings this evening.

WOMAN You'll have to explain to me what you were doing in that clock. (*To* BURGLAR) Was he in there when you were there?

BURGLAR (*After a moment's perplexity*) Well it's hard to say. It's very dark inside.

MAN It's all clear now, totally clear, just give me a minute and I'll clear up the misunderstanding. Well then...

BURGLAR Well...O help! There's no misunderstanding. It's like this. Now...

*Before he has time to go on, the others, afraid that he will uncover their individual affairs, interrupt hurriedly*

ANNA Of course there's been a misunderstanding... obviously there has.

ANTONIO Yes I understood that at once. In fact I'm

astonished that our friend here hasn't gathered that yet. It's all one big misunderstanding.

WOMAN   It's so clear that even a child could understand it.

MAN   So there's really no need of explanations. You can't explain misunderstandings, otherwise it would hardly be a misunderstanding, would it?

BURGLAR   (*To his* WIFE) Come on, let's get out.

BURGLAR'S WIFE   Just a minute. Don't pull me like that.

BURGLAR   Let's go before they notice.

*As they pass the switch, the* BURGLAR *puts out the light*

ANNA   Who's put out the light?

WOMAN   What's going on?

ANTONIO   Stop them! Where are those two off to?

WOMAN   He's so crazy he might even go off and give himself up . . . this minute.

MAN   Quick, stop them, don't let them get away.

WOMAN   They've gone out through the garden . . . run.

MAN   It's impossible. You two go out that way. You come with me.

*They all go out. Silence. From the window appears the light of a torch. The light comes right into the room and stops on the bag filled with the* BURGLAR'S *takings. At that point the others return.*

SECOND BURGLAR   Nice place here, the cutlery already parcelled up. Very thoughtful of them. (*Pause*) Somebody's coming.

MAN   He's come back in through the window, the scoundrel. He actually came back to get the silverware.

ANNA   Grab him.

WOMAN   Quick . . . hold him . . . don't let him get away.

ANNA   Switch on the light.

*When the light comes on, a* SECOND BURGLAR, *surrounded by his four pursuers, is seen*

ANNA   That's not the great Tornati. It's another one!

SECOND BURGLAR   Ah no, no. This is a bit much. You're starting to lay traps, leaving the window open, the loot all tied up and ready...and then just as I'm about to move, Bang! It's a fair cop Guv! No, that's just not playing the game. I'm going to see my union about this, so I'll bid you all good night.

EVERYONE   Noooooo!

MAN   No, for goodness' sake, listen, there's been a misunderstanding.

SECOND BURGLAR   A what?

EVERYONE   Misunderstanding.

MAN   Now, with your permission, we'll explain everything.

EVERYONE   It's like this...

*The following lines are to be spoken simultaneously, so that there will be a great din without a single word being understood*

WOMAN   Earlier this evening I was with my husband. I got a phone call and came here at once...

ANNA   I was at Villa Ponente. The phone rang and at the other end I heard a woman's voice insulting me...

MAN   I was at my mother's. We were just sitting down to eat when all of a sudden I remembered I'd left the office keys at home...

ANTONIO   I was at the cinema earlier on. The usual stuff, sex and violence, when...

*The SECOND BURGLAR, assaulted by the clamour of voices and meaningless words, moves back until he bumps into the sofa. He sits, then falls full length at the mercy of the four unfaithful liars who talk and talk and talk.*

*Blackout*

# Study activities

## Sorry, Wrong Number

**1** Look again at the stage directions at the beginning of the play. Discuss the impressions you form of Mrs Stevenson before she speaks.

**2** The play is obviously American. But apart from the names of places, how else can you tell? Discuss any other clues you can find in the language.

**3** Working in pairs or a small group, design a graph to show how the suspense builds at different points in the play. Put the main events of the plot along the horizontal axis and use the vertical axis to show how the tension rises or falls at each stage. At which point does the tension begin to build? How does it develop? How does the writer keep the audience in suspense? Use your chart to discuss tension in the play.

**4** One criticism of melodrama is that it relies too heavily on unbelievable characters and coincidence – in other words, we cannot really feel that the characters would exist as real people and too many events seem to just 'happen' without real explanation. Do you find that in this play? Which points in the play do you find least convincing?

**5** Imagine the final Operator discussing the conversation she has just had with Mrs Stevenson. What impressions has she made? How does she explain Mrs Stevenson's behaviour? Write a monologue showing us inside the Operator's mind.

**6** *Sorry, Wrong Number* has been produced as a television drama. How would you use editing of scenes and camera work to build tension? Plot out how you would place one scene after another, whether you would vary the locations more than in the original version, whether you would *show* all the operators, or just allow the audience to *hear* them, as Mrs Stevenson does. Which actors might play which parts? Write a detailed account of how you would produce the play for television.

**7** Write your own thriller in which the starting-point is a telephone call.

## Greenheart and the Dragon Pollutant

**1** The opening of the play says that the tale 'is based on an old mummers' play'. What do you know in your group about the tradition of the mummers' plays? Do some research using reference books, and present the results to the rest of the class.

**2** Who do you think is the intended audience for this play? What age-group does it best suit? What clues are there in the language of the play about the writer's intended audience?

**3** This is obviously a play with a message. How would you summarise the message in one phrase or sentence? Discuss whether you think the play is effective in conveying that message to its intended audience. How could it convey it more powerfully?

**4** Sometimes when characters have labels rather than names (for example Storyteller, Dragon, Doctor 1, and so on), the audience finds it difficult to feel sympathy for the characters. Does that happen in this play? Do we feel involved with the characters, on the side of the 'good' characters and opposed to the 'bad' ones? How successfully does the play involve its audience?

**5** Do some research about the origins of English drama – Mystery Plays and Morality Plays – and write an essay describing how the plays were rehearsed and performed.

**6** Imagine you are a theatre critic and you have just watched a performance of this play. Write a review for a local newspaper giving a flavour of the play, and discussing its strengths and weaknesses.

**7** A longer-term project: choose an issue you feel strongly about – for example drug abuse, the environment, crime – and write your own community play aimed at persuading the audience to your point of view. Then write a brief commentary describing the approach you took, the decisions you made and your feeling about the final result.

## A Thing of Beauty

**1** Look closely at the relationship between Sister Benedicta and the Colonel. How are their characters different? Do they have any similarities? How does the relationship develop during the play?

**2** Sister Benedicta says: 'You are like a parrot, Colonel. You spew the party line faithfully.' Discuss what motivates him: is he simply an evil man? Is he merely obeying orders? Is he doing what he genuinely believes to be right? Find evidence from the play to support your point of view.

**3** What do Sister Benedicta and the Colonel 'learn' from their encounter?

**4** The origins of the word *drama* lie in the Greek word *dran* meaning 'to do'. Drama, in other words, was something in which things happened. Read the following opinion of *A Thing of Beauty* and discuss whether you agree with it:

> The play is a lengthy dialogue about good and evil, love, and power. But it cannot really be called drama. Drama needs action, development, a stronger sense of real people in real places. Here the characters represent ideas rather than seeming to be real people.

**5** What would the Prioress's thoughts be as she thinks about what has happened as a result of her 'confession'? Write a monologue or diary, or create a role-play, in which we see her thoughts.

**6** Write as if you are the Colonel thinking back to your encounter with Sister Benedicta. Write about your first impressions of her, how your attitude towards her develops and changes, and the effect of the Prioress's information. Use your account to show the tensions in the Colonel's character.

**7** Write a critical essay about the play, examining how it is structured, how Charles Kray builds tension, what we learn of the characters, and how effective the ending is. Use quotations to support your ideas. Your title might be: 'A Personal Response to *A Thing of Beauty*'.

**8** Write your own play about an encounter between two people of strongly opposing viewpoints, who change or develop during the drama.

# Dead End

**1** Look back at the beginning of the play. At what point do you begin to detect that beneath the polite surface conversation, there is something more menacing?

**2** Brian Wedmore makes a series of points which hint that something suspicious is going on – such as the fact that Arabella's mother is never seen in the village. Make a list of other evidence that things are not as they should be.

**3** Both characters in the play behave in ways which seem strange or unexpected. Discuss each character in turn, saying what they are like, what is unusual about their attitudes or behaviour, and whether there are any parts of their personalities that you find unbelievable. You might use hot-seating to cross-examine each character.

**4** How do you explain the ending of the play? Why do we hear the mother's voice? Why does Brian become so angry as to attack Arabella?

**5** What would happen next in the play? Devise a role-play or script that continues the story.

**6** How does Richard Parsons create suspense in this play? Look at the way the characters behave, the questions he leaves unanswered and the way he plants hints of violence. Then write up your notes, giving specific examples from the play to support your observations.

**7** Compare *Dead End* with Lucille Fletcher's play *Sorry, Wrong Number*. What similarities do they have in characterisation, setting, use of tension and presentation of women? Write an essay comparing the two plays.

## Skin

**1** Reading a screenplay is different from reading the text of a stage play. What differences did you notice in the reading process during your first encounter with *Skin*? How did it prove more difficult than reading a conventional script?

**2** Who are the two main characters of the play? What are they like? What is, and was, their relationship? Why has it changed? Spend some time discussing and working out your answers to these questions posed by the text.

**3** One critic has described *Skin* as 'a play about the "issue" of disability which could almost be mistaken for a poignant teenage romance'. Discuss this statement. How does it change any of your reactions to the screenplay?

**4** How would the text translate into screen images? Take one scene and produce a storyboard to show how the words and images would combine.

**5** *Skin* is a challenging and disturbing screenplay. Write a personal response to it, discussing the characters, the themes and the story it tells. Illustrate your comments with brief quotations.

**6** How would you direct the screenplay? Who would you cast in the roles? What would different scenes look like? Write an informative essay explaining how you would approach the text as a director, and explaining the kind of problems you would need to overcome.

**7** Take one of the other plays in this collection and rewrite one scene as a screenplay. What changes are required to characterisation, stage directions and structure? Write a commentary on the process.

# Trouble in the Works

**1** Make notes on the characters of Fibbs and Wills. How should they behave? What advice would you give to actors playing each part about body language, dress, manner of speaking? What background information about each character could you provide?

**2** Look at the way Fibbs reacts to Wills's account of the workers' complaints. Discuss why he finds the news so 'shattering'.

**3** What makes this sketch funny? Look at the list below and discuss which elements you think add most to the overall humour of the sketch, placing them in order of most to least comic:

- the suggestive names of the factory machinery
- the serious tone of Wills and Fibbs
- the repetition of each character's dialogue
- the way the drama builds up from a slow start to a rapid conclusion
- the fact that Mr Fibbs seems genuinely upset by Wills's news.

Add any further points which seem important.

**4** What might happen next? Continue the dialogue between Fibbs and Wills, and perhaps take Mr Fibbs to visit the workers.

**5** Write a comic sketch in which one character breaks bad news to the other.

# Kitty

**1** Work in pairs to practise reading these two monologues aloud. Take turns to be Kitty and make suggestions to each other about:

- expression
- accent
- pace
- facial expressions
- pauses.

**2** With a monologue, we learn about a character from the words he or she uses – we have no one else's responses to guide our opinions. Make a list of the main features of Kitty's character. Then discuss whether you like her or not, and why.

**3** Victoria Wood uses place names to give Kitty a strongly northern identity – Cheadle, Widnes, Nantwich. They are also often places associated with middle rather than working classes. Look carefully at other references in Kitty's monologues – to people, places and objects – and discuss what they show us about her outlook on life.

**4** Write notes to an actress who is about to perform one of the Kitty monologues. Introduce her character, describe her attitude, give suggestions for the way she should dress, sit and behave, and for how certain lines should be spoken.

**5** Write your own monologue in which the character of the speaker is revealed only through the words they say. For ideas you might first read some monologues by Alan Bennett or Michael Frayn.

# The Still Alarm

**1** Read again through the opening part of the play. At which point did you begin to sense that this was not a realistic drama, that there was something 'odd' about it?

**2** One criticism of absurdist drama is that it sacrifices characterisation for dramatic effect – in other words, the characters are neither believable nor very interesting but simply serve the plot. Is that true of *The Still Alarm*? Look in particular at the characters of Ed and Bob and discuss what we learn about them. Are they believable?

**3** Do you find the play funny as a whole, or certain parts of it? Discuss what amused you during your reading, and discuss your response with others in the class. Try to define precisely what it was that amused you.

**4** How would the storyline have been different if this was a realistic play? At what point would it have altered from the version here? Write about the way the play would have developed if the fire had been taken seriously. You might write this as an alternative script.

**5** Imagine you are a theatre critic who is reviewing the play. What are its strengths and weaknesses? Focus on the following:

- characters
- plot
- language
- humour
- entertainment value.

**6** Write your own absurdist drama, in which events and dialogue are not what we might expect. For ideas you might read Ionesco's play *Rhinoceros*, in which a huge rhinoceros unexpectedly terrorises a sleepy French village.

## Teeth

**1** Find a recording of Bach's Toccata in C minor, and practise reading the play to the music. Discuss how the characters should play their parts, what tone of voice they should use, what attitude they have to one another.

**2** The play was written by an American writer. How can you tell from reading the play that it is American? Find different forms of evidence in the characters' choice of words, phrasing, and the way they are presented. Then discuss how the play would be different if the characters spoke with more obviously English patterns of speech.

**3** Some people find the ending of the play rather an anticlimax; they feel that it simply 'fades out'. Other critics might suggest that the conclusion is just right: it shows that the two characters *have* something in common after all, that they are less isolated than at the beginning of the play. Discuss your response to the ending.

**4** Write two character studies, one for Amy, one for Dr Rose. Bring out their similarities and differences, some observations about their attitudes and language, and illustrate your points with brief examples from the play.

**5** What happens next in *Teeth*? Continue the play, maintaining the style and characterisation as closely as you can.

# The Virtuous Burglar

**1** Like all farces, the plot of *The Virtuous Burglar* becomes more and more tangled as the plot develops. Working in a small group, invent a diagram or chart which shows how the storyline is organised.

**2** One regular criticism of farces is their reliance on coincidence – events happening in a way that we cannot really accept as realistic. Make a list of the coincidences which take place in this play, and the results they have (the first two examples are given to get you started). Then discuss whether you think the play relies too much upon coincidence.

| Coincidence | Result |
|---|---|
| The Man and Woman arrive at the flat while the Burglar is still there . . . | The Burglar finds himself getting involved in their relationship. |
| The Burglar's Wife telephones and the Man answers the call . . . | |

**3** Use these prompts to discuss your reaction to the play overall:

- The most interesting character was . . .
- The funniest moment in the play was . . .
- The part I found most difficult to follow was . . .
- The character I least liked was . . .
- The play would have been more enjoyable if . . .
- My overall opinion of the play was . . .

**4** The play was written and first perfomed in Italy. How important is that setting? Would the play entertain an audience wherever it was performed, or are there some aspects of the humour which you think would not travel well?

**5** Based on your discussion work, write a detailed response to *The Virtuous Burglar*. Discuss your reaction to two different characters, the structure of the play, the way the plot develops, the use of coincidence, and the conclusion. Illustrate your points, where possible, with brief quotations from the text.

**6** What challenges would the play pose to a theatre director? What would be required from the actors and set-designer? In his absurdist drama, George S. Kaufman said that *The Still Alarm* should be acted 'calmly and politely, in the manner of an English drawing-room comedy'. How should *The Virtuous Burglar* be played – manically, seriously, purely for laughs?

Write as if you were about to direct the play, providing initial notes for different members of the theatre company. Make your advice as specific as possible.

# The authors

**Nicola Batty**. *Skin* was written as a result of the BBC's *Debut on Two* competition, which aimed to discover writers who had not previously written for television. Submissions had to last no more than fifteen minutes. *Skin* was one of the eight winning entries and was subsequently filmed and shown on BBC television.

**Lucille Fletcher** was born in Brooklyn, New York in 1913. She wrote a number of novels, radio and television plays. *Sorry, Wrong Number* was first written as a novel, and has since been adapted as a radio play, film (in 1948), television play and – included here – stage play.

**Dario Fo** was born in Lombardy, Italy, in 1926 and began his theatrical career as an actor and director, and writer of satirical comedies. In the 1960s he found a wider audience than in the traditional theatre, writing political comedies for performance in factories and workers' clubs.

**Tina Howe** is the author of several plays, for which she has won a number of awards. She was born in New York in 1937 and teaches at New York University.

**George S. Kaufman** worked as a journalist, director and screenwriter well-known for his lighthearted comedies. He was one of the most successful playwrights of the 1920s and 1930s, usually in collaboration with other writers, such as Moss Hart, with whom he wrote *The Man Who Came to Dinner* (1939). He was born in Pittsburgh, Pennsylvania in 1889 and died in 1961.

**Charles Kray** is an actor and director as well as a writer. He worked for a time as a staff writer and director with Universal Studios in Hollywood.

**Cressida Miles** wrote *Greenheart and the Dragon Pollutant* as an entry for the Sacred Earth Drama Trust drama competition. This contest invited writers to produce original dramas on an ecological theme. Cressida Miles's work was highly commended.

**Richard Parsons**. Sir Richard worked for the British Diplomatic Service as Ambassador to Spain, Sweden and Hungary. He was born in 1928 and is the author of several novels and plays.

**Harold Pinter** was born in London in 1930 and began his professional career as an actor. His early work baffled audiences: critics called *The Birthday Party* (1958) 'half-gibberish' and 'a baffling mixture'. The word 'Pinteresque' has since evolved to describe his style – drama in which a sense of menace frequently lies beneath the surface dialogue.

**Victoria Wood** is the writer and star of several television series. She was born in 1953, and after a degree in Drama at Birmingham University she began her career as a stand-up comedian, focusing on the ordinary details of life. As one critic has said: 'Her observations are merciless and acute, and it's the marriage of northern and southern humour which gives her work such an interesting perspective.'

# Further reading

The best way to develop your enthusiasms and interest in plays is to visit the theatre regularly. Most theatres offer discount tickets to young people, helping you to see a variety of plays at reduced prices. For specific reading within the various styles and genres represented within this collection of plays, the following are particularly recommended.

## Thrillers and melodrama

See Joseph Kesselring's *Arsenic and Old Lace* (English Theatre, 1990), Agatha Christie's *The Mousetrap* (Collins, 1993) and Frederick Knott's *Dial M for Murder* (Samuel French, 1992) as classic examples of this genre.

## Community theatre

This form of theatre has to be experienced rather than read, but some lively scripts can convey some of its flavour – for example Ann Jellicoe: *The Knack* (Methuen, 1961), David Edgar: *The Life and Adventures of Nicholas Nickleby* (Methuen, 1980), and any play by John Godber, but especially *Bouncers* (Methuen, 1980), about life in northern nightclubs.

## Tragedy

Sophocles' *Oedipus* trilogy makes gripping reading, especially in Timberlake Wertenberke's adaptation for the

Royal Shakespeare Company: *The Thebans* (Faber, 1992).
Shakespeare's most accessible tragedy is *Macbeth*, in which
we trace a heroic figure's decline to disaster. Arthur Miller's
*The Crucible, Death of a Salesman* (both Penguin, 1989) and
*A View from the Bridge* (Penguin, 1990) are all powerful
tragedies set in small American communities.

## TV screenplays

A good introduction to the genre is *Debut on Two* (edited
by P. Giles and V. Lickorish, BBC Books, 1990), which
contains essays by screenwriters on their techniques. Also
recommended: Dennis Potter's *The Singing Detective* (Faber,
1986) and Jack Rosenthal's *Wide-Eyed and Legless*
(Longman, 1995).

## Sketches

Particularly recommended are: Victoria Wood's *Barmy*
(Methuen, 1987) and *Up to You, Porky* (Methuen, 1988),
collected from her television series. Harold Pinter's revue
sketches are contained in *Plays Two* (Faber, 1991). Michael
Frayn's *Listen to This* (Methuen, 1990) also contains many
comic monologues and duologues. For monologues
specifically, see Joyce Grenfell's hilarious *George, Don't Do
That* (Macmillan, 1977) and Alan Bennett's *Talking Heads*
(BBC Books, 1988).

## Absurdism

Samuel Beckett's early plays show this form of theatre at its
most darkly baffling, especially *Waiting for Godot* (Faber,
1956), *Happy Days* (Faber, 1966) and *Endgame* (Faber,
1958). Much more purely comic, while still absurd, are

N. F. Simpson's plays, which enjoyed a revival on the London stage in the late 1980s – especially *One-Way Pendulum* (Samuel French, 1992).

## Comedy/Farce

Comedy is a difficult dramatic form within which to make suggestions: what is humorous to one person may not be so to another. Modern comic plays which contain elements of farce include: Alan Ayckbourn's *Absurd Person Singular* (Longman, 1989), Dario Fo's *Plays One* (Methuen, 1992), Ben Elton's *Gasping* (Sphere, 1990). For a more extreme brew of farce, see plays by Georges Feydeau, Ray Cooney, and Joe Orton's dark farce *Loot* (Methuen, 1973). From television, see the collection of scripts from *Fawlty Towers* by John Cleese and Connie Booth (Methuen, 1988).

# Further reading projects

1. Choose one of the styles of drama that you have enjoyed and write a comparison of two or three different plays. Focus on the characters, structure of the plot and use of language.

2. Choose a play you have both read and seen performed. Write an account of the performance, showing the decisions and interpretations made by the theatre company. Were there any points in the performance where you disagreed with any of the decisions that had been made?

3. Choose a play you have particularly enjoyed reading and write an account of how you would direct it. Discuss setting, casting and style.

Pearson Education Limited
*Edinburgh Gate, Harlow,*
*Essex CM20 2JE, England*
*and Associated Companies throughout the world.*

This educational edition first published 1996
Sixth impression 2004

*Editorial material set in 10/12.5 Stone Sans*
*Printed in Malaysia, PA*

ISBN 0 582 25383 7

The publisher's policy is to use paper manufactured from sustainable forests

**Acknowledgements**
We are grateful to the following copyright holders for permission to reproduce plays:

Faber & Faber Ltd for 'Trouble in the Works' by Harold Pinter from *A Slight Ache and Other Plays*; the William Morris Agency, Inc on behalf of the author, Lucille Fletcher for 'Sorry Wrong Number'. Copyright (c) 1948 by Lucille Fletcher; Samuel French, Inc for 'The Still Alarm' by George S Kaufman. Copyright (c) 1925 by George S Kaufman. Copyright (c) 1930 by Brady & Wiman Productions Corporation. Copyright (c) 1952 (in renewal) by George S Kaufman. Copyright (c) 1957 (in renewal) by George S Kaufman; the playwright Charles Kray for his 'A Thing of Beauty'; the author's agents for 'Dead End' by Richard Parsons, publ. Samuel French Ltd, London 1994. (Application for amateur rights should be made to them at 52 Fitzroy Street, London W1P 6JR. before rehearsals commence); Reed Consumer Books Ltd for 'The Virtuous Burlgar' by Dario Fo, translated by Jo Farrell, first published in *Plays One* by Methuen Drama 1992. Text © 1992 Jo Farrell. The Translator has asserted her moral rights. All rights reserved; Sacred Earth Drama Trust for 'Greenheart and the Dragon Pollutant' by Cressida Miles in *Sacred Earth Dramas* publ Faber & Faber Ltd, 1993.

We have unfornately been unable to trace the copyright holders of 'Skin' by Nicola Batty, 'Teeth' by Tina Howe, and would appreciate any information which would enable us to do so.

Cover illustration by Debbie Lush
Cover design by Ship

Cover illustration: Scene 1 of *Skin*